CHRISTIAN ENCOUNTERS

SAINT
FRANCIS

CHRISTIAN ENCOUNTERS

SAINT FRANCIS

ROBERT WEST

THOMAS NELSON
Since 1798

NASHVILLE   DALLAS   MEXICO CITY   RIO DE JANEIRO

FOR MY FATHER,
EARL WEST

A prolific writer of biographies and histories,
whose integrity, compassion, faith,
and devotion to truth
have been a lifelong inspiration to me.

Published in Nashville, Tennessee, by Thomas Nelson. Thomas Nelson is a registered trademark of Thomas Nelson, Inc.

Represented by *WordServe Literary Group, Ltd*. Greg Johnson, Literary Agent.

Thomas Nelson, Inc., titles may be purchased in bulk for educational, business, fund-raising, or sales promotional use. For information, please e-mail SpecialMarkets@ThomasNelson.com.

Unless otherwise noted, Scripture quotations are taken from the HOLY BIBLE: NEW INTERNATIONAL VERSION®. © 1973, 1978, 1984 by International Bible Society. Used by permission of Zondervan Publishing House. All rights reserved.

Scripture quotations marked KJV are from the KING JAMES VERSION.

Scripture quotations marked NEB are from THE NEW ENGLISH BIBLE. © 1961. 1970 by The Delegates of the Oxford University Press and the Syndics of the Cambridge University Press. Reprinted by permission.

Library of Congress Cataloging-in-Publication Data

West, Robert, 1945–
  Saint Francis / by Robert West.
    p. cm.
  Includes bibliographical references.
  ISBN 978-1-59555-107-8
  1. Francis, of Assisi, Saint, 1182-1226. 2. Christian saints—Italy—Assisi—Biography. 3. Assisi (Italy)—Biography. I. Title.
  BX4700.F6W38 2010
  271'.302--dc22
  [B]
    2010010462

Printed in the United States of America
10 11 12 13 HCI 6 5 4 3 2 1

CONTENTS

1

OUT OF THE NIGHT

The city bustled into the morning much as it did every day. Carts rattled and wagons rumbled along the unpaved streets, stirring up chickens and spooking dogs and horses that happened to be in the way. From the crowing of cocks to the bleating of sheep and the laughing of children as they ran about riding broomstick warhorses, a cacophony of sounds intruded upon every conversation.

Amid this turmoil of sight and sound, the wisp of another sound—of someone shouting (or was it singing?) emanated from the mist below the city gate to the east. A few people on the outer reaches of the piazza turned to look, but the sound was mostly lost as farmers and craftsmen began hawking their wares and criers called out the virtues of this and that product. The voices of people, instead of traffic noises, still prevailed in the streets eight centuries ago—itinerant salesmen shouting "Get your pots and jars here!" as they rambled along in carts or walked the streets wrapped in their wares. Peddlers jangled their bells, calling out "for sale or trade" to draw attention to their baskets filled with jewelry.[1]

That other voice was becoming louder and more obtrusive. More people swung about and peered into the harsh glare of the rising sun. Yes, there was someone there—a small shadow of a man, with the outline of a church at his back, half walking and half dancing.

Church bells all over the city had already called the population to early mass—"prime" it was called in the circuit of hours for the church, set at about six o'clock, except, of course, there were no clocks in those days. Everyone went to mass. Heaven and hell were too vividly envisioned in the medieval mind to ignore the entreaties of faith.

The voice, which sounded so dissonant against the clamoring city, grew louder, attracting the attention of an increasing number of people. Soon they were able to see a disheveled and emaciated young man coming toward them, his hair and beard coarse and untended, his movements erratic. In reality he was forced to hop this way and that to avoid the pigs, flocks of sheep, goats, and other animals, which were allowed to roam freely to clean the streets of accumulated garbage. Rarely just walking, he frequently broke into a run or even spun around with his hands held high.

His features still lost in the morning mist, those nearest to him could now discern that he was singing. Having neither radios nor any other entertainment devices, shopkeepers, craftsmen, and ladies hanging out the wash frequently sang to themselves as they worked—usually the songs made popular by traveling troubadours, *jongleurs*, and minstrels.[2]

These were not the kind of songs the strange man was singing, however. The words "God," "Lord," and "praise" stood out from the others. He leaped again into the air, shouting something incomprehensible. This time, though, as he landed, he slipped in the mud and fell onto all fours. It had rained the previous day, so that the various components of the reeking discharge on the streets were being churned into a very unpleasant muck. He was back up immediately, however, resuming his shouting and singing as if nothing had happened. Murmurs began arising from the milling crowd. Somebody called out "Madman!" Other voices echoed similar phrases as the *giovani*, or young man, rushed awkwardly through the flow of street vendors and shoppers. He looked for all the world like a beggar, except that beneath the layer of dirt was a relatively expensive tunic. His face also did not express hunger or hardship but held a strange expression of exultation. He sang worship songs in ringing tones of ecstasy, his praises shouted up to God the way people usually yelled to urge their men on during games or jousts.

"A religious freak," some onlookers grumbled in disgust. People wondered if he might be a member of one of those heretical religious sects that were popping up here and there. One called *Ordo Penitentium*, "the penitential order," had been gaining attention of late.[3]

His expression of happiness clashed with his unhealthful and beggarly appearance, drawing more catcalls denigrating his sanity and intelligence. Then someone recognized the face. The news spread through the crowd like an ocean wave.

It was a startling revelation. He was known all over town as one of the wild youths who frequently disturbed the peace of the city—a notorious profligate who, along with his similarly wild friends, was known for engaging in lavish and bawdy parties, carousing drunkenly through the streets late at night.

Madness! That was the only explanation. Jeering voices began to rise from among the crowd at seeing this high and mighty peacock so fallen. The tenor of turmoil amplified as the younger crowd began pelting him with disgusting mud clods. Others gathered around him and began pushing and shoving him about. He'd been a gang leader of sorts, and rivals seized this opportunity to prey upon him. They knocked him about, circling him as if they were baiting a bear, beating him mercilessly.

He was passed raucously from one group of persecutors to another along the winding street that climbed toward the piazza. Proving his madness, during all of this raucous mistreatment his look of happiness lingered.

His name was Francesco, better known as Francis, and one day he would be proclaimed a saint.

THE MERCHANT
AND THE DREAMER

From his childhood, Francis had desired to be neither the son of a rich man nor a saint. These were the days of legends—of King Arthur and Percival, of Saint George and Roland and Charlemagne. Visions of knights in brilliant armor—rescuing beautiful ladies, making grand gestures of benevolence, dueling valiantly with the forces of evil, and bravely driving back the infidel from the borders of Christendom—danced in his imagination. With every breath in his body, he wanted to become a knight.

Most people blame his obsession with knights and their code of chivalry on his mother, Pica, who was from Provençal. That region in southern France is credited with giving birth to many of the *chansons de geste* or "songs of heroic deeds" that became famous throughout Europe. French was the language of the *jongleurs* and troubadours who sang or recited these stories, so it is natural to assume that Francis learned that language from his mother—specifically the dialect of Provençal.

There were more practical reasons for learning French, however. It was the language upon which his father's fortune was founded. Pietro di Bernadone was a merchant—a buyer, seller, and manufacturer of fine fabrics. The center of the cloth industry was in southern France, where the great trade fairs were held each year. Thanks to the market for fine fashions among the nobility and the increasingly prosperous middle class, Pietro had bought and sold and traded his way to considerable wealth through those fairs. Even the pending birth of his first child could not dissuade him from making the journey to them.

His father was therefore far away when Francis was born. Neighbors and family members and especially Pica had urged him to wait, but the fairs were essential to his prosperity—to the good life, he assured himself, that he was making for his wife and child.

In his absence, Pica had her baby christened at Assisi's cathedral, San Rufino, naming him John after John the Baptist. When Pietro returned, however, he was not pleased with his wife's choice of a name. The Baptist had been a hermit who lived in the wilderness in poverty—not at all the role model for the son of a prosperous merchant. He insisted that his boy's name be changed to Francis. That name was not common in Italy, for it means "the French one," but Pietro owed both his lovely French wife and his enviable livelihood to the people of that land beyond the Alps.

Francis therefore, as they say, grew up in the lap of luxury. Thomas of Celano, in his 1230 biography, the first written about

Francis, accuses his parents of leading him into a life driven by a desire for worldly pleasures, suggesting that their worldly behavior provided a poor example for the boy to follow.

Apparently, then as now, the parent tended to bear the brunt of blame for an unruly child. Thomas also criticizes them for being lax in discipline. Discipline at that time included a liberal use of the "rod," including an occasional beating. Given Pietro's reputation, as well as his treatment of Francis during the period of his conversion, it is doubtful that he was negligent in exacting discipline either with or without the rod.

Rearing a child was just as complex eight hundred years ago as it has always been. Thomas admits that if children "behave virtuously, they become subjected to harsh punishments," meaning bullying, taunting, and fighting at school, on street corners, and in the piazzas. Another of Thomas's comments will ring a timely bell with anyone who has ever been a teenager: "Children talk about doing worse things than they actually do, so that they will not be perceived as more innocent."[1]

Thomas met Francis and became one of his followers, but the men spent very little time together. Consequently, when Thomas was commissioned by Pope Gregory IX in 1228 to write the biography, he had to rely upon the testimony of others who had known or shared experiences with Francis during the various phases of his life, filling in the blanks with his own conclusions. After the release of his biography, Thomas heard that Pica, now a widow, was hurt and offended by his portrayal of her. He made further inquiries and discovered that she was a spiritually minded person who may have quietly nurtured the spiritual in Francis. Thomas, in fact, discovered enough new information that he wrote another biography in 1247. His *Second Life*, as it is called, not only presents Pica in a much more favorable light, but appends his *First Life of St. Francis*, as it became called, with corrections and additional material.

Neither of Thomas's biographies provides much detail about Francis's formative years. In all ages, of course, children play. Most of the toys children played with in the twelfth century were improvised from sticks or stones or household items. Children from wealthier families, like Francis, might have had store-bought toys. Francis probably wouldn't have been interested in the porcelain dolls, but he would have begged for the tiny horses with riders—probably enough of them to engage in a sizable miniature battle. Like many children, Francis preferred playing to eating. When summoned by a voice outside, he'd immediately rush off, leaving a tremor of cups and plates and the groans of his parents in his wake.

Francis had a younger brother named Angelo about whom we know little. We can assume that they occasionally played together, although older brothers often prefer friends to little brothers. Most of the games they played sound roughly familiar: hide-and-seek, catch, or, by adding a stick, a primitive form of street hockey or soccer. Added to these were the improvisations of their imagination. A stick, raised high with a war cry, turns into Excalibur, and a longer stick held by a boy riding a broomstick horse transforms the game into a joust. In the winter they threw snowballs and, on a less appetizing note, took the bladders of slaughtered pigs to blow up into balloons.[2]

Like virtually all people in that day, Francis went to church at least once a day, most often with his mother since his father spent so much time away from home. Like most children, he enjoyed hearing stories from the Bible but otherwise took religion pretty much for granted.

Play time became increasingly limited as a boy grew older. As early as age eight, a child might be required to help in his father's business. Rarely in those days did people have separate buildings for work and living. The shop would be on the ground floor of the house with business carried on mostly in the street in front of the house. The seller might lay a board across supports to display goods, or a counter could be built into the house at the base of a large window (not yet including glass) with shelves inside for storage. The shop was usually at the front of a long room with the kitchen and eating area in the rear, so that family members could keep an eye on the shop while they were eating.

The narrow city streets were generally packed with traffic—largely pedestrian. Streets in those days were for people, not modes of transportation. They allowed individuals to move from shop to shop doing business. Carts and wagons had to fight through the crowds as best they could. Different kinds of businesses occupied different streets or neighborhoods—carpenters on one street, jewelry makers in another area, with places for tanning hides in another. Shopkeepers and artisans advertised their wares by hiring criers to walk about calling out their offerings. These criers were a generally disreputable lot that could be found hanging out in taverns and gaming houses.

People spent a lot of time out of doors. Houses were small—hot and stuffy in the summer, cold and drafty in the winter. With no refrigerators for keeping food, people had to go out and shop every day. Everyone knew everyone else, and people could sit and rest or talk on stone benches, which were placed along the streets in front of the shops/houses. Rows of porticos (porches) offered shelter from rain, as did overhanging roofs. Umbrellas weren't due to come along until the sixteenth century. A major reason, in fact, for the streets being so narrow and winding was to help protect pedestrians from the sun and the wind.[3]

Young Francis helped out by moving stock around and fetching and carrying whatever his father wished. Word was that Pietro was fairly indulgent toward the boy when it came to teaching him the business. There was no question that his father had a keen eye for profits, but Pietro had a reputation for being temperamental and ruthless in his business dealings. Francis, who was expected to succeed his father in the family business, was of a different cloth—more good-natured and generous, perhaps pressing his father's irritability with an occasional price break to a needy person.

Many scholars believe that Francis grew up in a house on Chiesa Nuova, although the street wasn't given that name until the seventeenth century. It was only a block away from the city's main street, the *Via di Ceppo della Catena*, and a block east of the *Piazza del Commune*, the civic and commercial center of town. The main streets in Assisi ran laterally, essentially east to west, across the spur of Mt. Subasio, which loomed above the city to the northwest. The smaller streets, alleys, pathways, and archways crossed those streets, but rarely at anything close to a right angle.

Houses were distributed unevenly along the narrow streets, some protruding into the street by several feet, giving the streets a jagged configuration. Holy images were illuminated at night, but the streets were generally dark anyway, made more so by the occasional archway and the roofs, created of terra-cotta tiles, overhanging the streets.[4] In addition, since Assisi was built on the side of a mountain, one might be required to traverse an occasional shallow flight of steps on the way to the market.

Like most buildings and houses in Assisi as well as the city's walls and gates, Pietro di Bernadone's house was built of stone quarried from Mount Subasio. The stone tended to give the city a slightly pinkish tinge at sunset, which faded to a pale gray under the moonlight.

The ground floor of the Bernadone house was vaulted and, as well as containing the shop, could be used as a storeroom or stable—the horse, donkey, and cows providing the upper floors with a modicum of heat at night. Next to the stable door was a smaller one, higher from the ground, which allowed access to the living quarters above. There was little privacy in those days. While the houses of the nobility might offer separate bedrooms, most families slept all in one room, several to a bed. Every night the wood steps to the living quarters were pulled up into the house. Assisi was not a safe place after dark.[5]

In those days most never learned to read and write and, since the two were not usually taught together as they are today, many knew only how to read or write, not both. Merchant families, of course, had to be educated in reading, writing, and mathematics. Consequently Francis began attending school, like most children in his social class, at the age of seven. Girls went to school, too, but were typically occupied in learning how to spin, embroider, weave, knit, and sew—the tasks required for a good housekeeper and wife.[6]

The school was located at the church of San Giorgio in an open space on the lower, far eastern side of the city—actually outside the city wall. Lessons began after Easter and were held in the atrium of the church. Vines and climbing flowers on the columns and arches made for a pleasant learning environment. The priest's chief priority was to make sure that the children learned the great stories of the Bible and the saints. Like most boys, Francis probably paid particular attention to the heroes and battles of the Bible. Beyond that, the boys were taught the seven "liberal arts," most important among them being grammar, dialectic, and rhetoric. Given his later success as a preacher, Francis may have excelled particularly in the latter subject. Waxed tablets or boards were used for writing.

Going to school wasn't necessarily a pleasant experience. The "rod" was considered essential for education and was applied without hesitation. The boys were taught Italian—the Umbrian dialect—and how to write, translate, and speak Latin, which was the universal language of the educated in Europe. Dialectic was intended to train the young how to think and argue logically based upon reason, authority, or experience.

Overall, it is doubtful that academic pursuits were of much interest to Francis. He was filled with dreams of flashing armor, beautiful ladies in flowing silk gowns, banners flying, and crowds cheering, all of which the troubadours sang. The subjects he learned at San Giorgio were of little use to a knight.

The knighthood that Francis sought, however, bore little resemblance to the real thing. The *chansons de geste* exalted the valor of combatants, their love for fair ladies, their loyalty, generosity, and courtesy. Francis apparently adopted several of these characteristics before he was even able to carry a sword. Thomas of Celano records that he developed such good manners that people mistook him for a born nobleman.

The troubadour songs that came from the courts of chivalry in southern France were, at first, based upon the legendary and occasionally real incidents in the history of France during the eighth and ninth centuries. Their heroes were Charles Martel and Charlemagne. The most well-known of these songs was the *Chanson de Roland*, or "Song of Roland." Legends from other countries, like the exploits of King Arthur and his Knights of the Round Table, were soon added. Troubadours traveled all over the countryside—to castles, villages, and city piazzas—singing about beautiful women and the infatuation of lovers. Some would take a bawdier slant, focusing upon a knight's desire that his lady would "lower her defenses."

Francis had many role models he could draw upon in song and legend. Even among the saints, the lore of the knight caught his attention. Francis became particularly fond of Saint Michael, who led the heavenly armies against the demons from hell. While attending school at San Giorgio, it is certainly possible that he gained an admiration for San Giorgio (Saint George), the knight who slew a dragon. On the feast of Saint George, it was customary for the knights of the city and the surrounding areas to hold jousts and tournaments.

The story, told every year in that church atrium, never failed to hold the children rapt to every delicious detail as they heard of a horrifying dragon that came out of the sea and terrorized a kingdom. Knights by the hundreds were sent to kill it, but all retreated in terror. The king thought that he could appease the dragon with a sacrifice—one of the maidens in the kingdom. The choice was made by lot and, to the king's great despair, his beautiful daughter was chosen. The day dawned for the sacrifice and the beautiful princess waited in terror for the dragon to come and devour her. But before that moment came, George arrived on his great horse and slew the beast. When George appeared before the king and the people, he preached to them the Christian faith. All were converted, churches were built, and the people were taught how to live the Christian life. The departure of George made a particular impression upon Francis, for he gave his noble horse and his armor to the poor for the love of Christ.

Some knights, like Percival, one of the Knights of the Round Table, had a strong spiritual side to them. San Rufino, the patron saint of Assisi, although not a knight, had a song dedicated to him, which included the refrain, "The martyr fights valiantly, like the lion, he does not know the meaning of defeat." Rufino had traveled throughout Italy during the third century, converting many to the new religion of Christ. He eventually settled in Assisi and became the town's first bishop. The Roman emperor, however, had no tolerance for Christianity and sometime between 236 and 239 ordered the proconsul of Assisi to torture Rufino with fire and threaten him with execution so that he would give up his religious intentions. But Rufino defied the proconsul, who subsequently ordered that he be thrown into the River Chiagio, just west of Assisi, with a millstone tied around his neck. The town's new cathedral, which crowned the city beneath the mountain, still under construction during Francis's life, was dedicated to his memory.

The Bernadone family may have been as wealthy as or even

wealthier than the noble families of the city, but they were not noble. Most knights were drawn from the nobility who were, as a class, professional warriors. That put Francis at a significant disadvantage in obtaining the skills required of a knight. Instead of attending school as Francis did, the sons of the nobility were raised on estates and castles in the countryside where they worked persistently at learning swordplay and the use of a shield, and practiced how to wield a lance and control a war horse.

Francis did have one advantage on his side: he had a very rich father. In earlier times, before the rise of a prosperous middle class, noble lords had been the only people who could afford to purchase the enormously costly equipment required for a knight. That was no longer the case. Pietro's vast wealth allowed the Bernadone family to emulate the lifestyle of the nobility. They even owned lands and estates in the country where Francis could spend time, when not required to work in the shop, practicing the skills of a knight. Not all noble houses were rolling in wealth, so his money may have convinced at least one noble boy to relax class barriers and be his tutor. Angelo of Tancredi, a noble house, might have been willing to help Francis on the basis of friendship, whether or not Francis offered him payment. We do not know that they were friends during their youth, but Angelo eventually gave up his noble heritage to become one of Francis's early followers and a devoted companion.

By the time Francis left school at age thirteen, the family had moved. No doubt an indication of Pietro's growing wealth, the family now lived in a house set on the main street between two churches, San Nicolo and San Paolo. Directly in front of the house were the Piazza del Commune and the market.[7] Just a skip down the street was a building fronted by a row of classical, fluted columns. This was the Temple of Minerva built during the time of Augustus, sometime before AD 14. It was now the property of the Benedictine monks of San Benedetto Abbey on the slope of Mount Subasio south of the city but would, in eight years or so, become the city's town hall. Pietro's new shop was at the center of Assisi's official business district. If there was such a thing as prime commercial real estate in Assisi, this had to be it.

Now Francis would hear the city heralds announcing the latest proclamations made by the magistrates. Following the blast of a trumpet, the town crier would announce upcoming meetings, issues before the court, and various changes in local laws as well as more interesting pieces of news concerning the empire, affairs in Florence and in Rome. Francis would also have a front-row view of the many festival processions and the ceremonies on election days.

Pietro's new house may also have had another symbol of wealth—a tower with turrets included.

Tower houses were the usual urban abode of the nobility. The countryside around Assisi was littered with castles and/or estates belonging to noble families, the greatest of these being La Rocca Maggiore, the fortress near the top of Mount Subasio, where the emperor often resided when in Umbria. The city had been expanding to control increasing areas of the surrounding countryside, prompting large landowners to move into the town, where they built large fortified houses for themselves.

Towers were, in fact, the dominating feature in Italian cities of the time. Perugia, Assisi's rival city fifteen miles away, reportedly once had more than five hundred tower houses. Even the smallest cities might have had as many as seventy such houses. The grandest of these homes, of course, belonged to the nobles in the upper part of the city who competed with one another for the tallest and most ostentatious towers.[8]

These houses weren't just for show, however; they were fortified against attack. Rivalries between families were commonplace all over Italy. Sometimes a tower served as a base from which to launch an attack against belligerent neighbors. Of the tower houses in Rome, it was said that the nobles sat in their tower castles and palaces "thirsting for battle in ruins on the classic hills as though Rome were not a city but an open territory the possession of which was to be disputed in daily warfare."[9]

Pietro's primary concern was to increase the family's wealth and prestige. In spite of Francis's expensive knighthood fantasy, Pietro had every expectation that his son would succeed him. After all, every physically fit man in Assisi, whatever his primary occupation, was expected to fight in defense of the city. Communes had, in fact, usurped the rights of feudal lords to confer knighthood. Francis, he thought, could play the part of a knight when necessary, while most of the time being a merchant like his father. When Francis turned fourteen, Pietro began in earnest to teach him the skills needed for work that his schooling had overlooked—how to use numbers, how to balance an account sheet, and how to evaluate the value of materials. He was drilled on the cloth business: how to recognize the quality of a bolt of cloth; how to distinguish types of twine, wools, weaves, and dyes; and where they could be found.

Pietro was also a manufacturer of cloth, which meant that Francis, in order to oversee workers, had to learn how the skilled craftsmen in his father's employ spun the raw wool into yarn and wove it into cloth. Wool was the favored material for clothing in the Middle Ages. It was expensive, but medieval spinners, weavers, and "finishing" specialists, which included those who applied dyes and fulling (giving cloth a shiny surface), were able to make several types of woolen cloth by using different grades of wool or by adjusting various steps in the manufacturing process. That way, they could produce cloth ranging from cheap, poorly finished fabrics to thick, luxurious cloths.

It is likely that, behind the counter in Pietro's house, toward the back of the house, instead of a kitchen and dining area, a cloth-making workshop was busy throughout the day. The living area was therefore dedicated to the upper floors. They may have even had the kitchen on the top floor. That arrangement benefited fire safety, but it was expensive since builders would have to carry all the construction materials up two or more flights of stairs. But then Pietro, the richest man in town, could afford it.

One aspect of the cloth trade that Francis may have enjoyed was journeying to the great commercial fairs in France. When his father thought he was old enough, say fifteen or sixteen, he may have let Francis come along. These trips could last from six weeks to three months, but they were essential to the family's prosperity, since the specialty of these fairs was the sale of cloth.

Assisi lay just off the principal road connecting Rome with France. It was called, appropriately enough, the *Strada Francesca*. Tradesmen and merchants constantly traveled that road, banding together in armed convoys for the journey.

They would have to take pack animals laden not only with provisions but with items that Pietro could trade—dyes, cloth samples, maybe even some leather goods and metal work crafted in and around Assisi.

Francis's mother no doubt wrung her hands in worry as they were preparing to leave, for it was a difficult journey, and the dangers were substantial. Hardly able to contain his excitement, Francis probably dropped into speaking French time and again as he prepared. Francis could trip into speaking French at any time, but especially when he was in an elevated state of excitement.[10] At such times he abandoned any concern for whether anyone could understand him or not.

Sometime, probably in June, they passed through the Sant'Antimo gate, the main city gate, riding in Pietro's wagon. With the pack animals tied behind the wagon, they took the old road to the Strada Francesca at the foot of the hill. There they met a caravan of merchants from Orvieto with whom they were to travel.[11] The road took them through Pisa and then up near Genoa, one of the major nodes for world trade. There Pietro may have stopped to acquire silk and spices from the East to use as trade items at the fair.

From there they traveled on to Milan and then looked toward the white-capped peaks of the Alps. The most popular routes dating back to Carolingian times were the Great Saint Bernard and Mont Cenis passes. Either way, the going was treacherous. There were few guides or hospices, and they slept mostly under canvas until the *caravanserais* (or roadside inns) were erected along the routes. Dangers from avalanches, wild animals, and sudden weather changes exacerbated the usual problems of travel. There were also the gangs of discharged mercenaries, known as *routiers*, who preyed upon the unwary along the trade routes. The convention known as the "Peace of God" had been instigated in Europe to protect priests, monks and hermits, the elderly, women and children, farmers, cowherds and laborers, as well as merchants. Of course, those omitted from this list did not offer as lucrative returns for their efforts, so the *routiers* generally ignored the convention.

The fairs were held in cycles, at various times in different cities throughout the year. The most famous of these were located in the Champagne region of southern France. First in the cycle was the Lagny fair in January/February. The next fair was held in Bar-sur Aube, followed by ones in Province and Troyes, the last being a second Troyes fair in November/December.[12]

The fairs were not free. Sellers generally paid a tax or fee to a landowner or count—whoever sponsored the event—for the space to sell their wares during the usual two-week period. In spite of the dangers and the cost, people came to the fairs from all over Europe and beyond.

Metal goods and salted fish were brought in from Lubeck, while bearded Russians from Novgorod brought bales of glossy furs—bear, wolf, beaver, fox, and marten. Spaniards contributed still more metal crafts. Caravans from the Middle East might also appear, bringing precious metals and spices and sometimes Arab horses. From the Baltic region came furs, honey, and forest products, and the British contributed tin and raw wool to exchange for highly prized Flemish cloth.

Cloth was the main contribution of the French, the primary focus of these fairs, and the item of most interest to Pietro.

Particularly appealing were the finest cloths, including the most resplendent silks, dyed scarlet or crimson—dyes created from the kermes insects bred and collected in the Mediterranean oak forests. Such cloth was greatly prized by the nobles of Assisi. For the same reason, Pietro may also have looked over the expensive silks and satin imported from the Middle East and the softest linens and cottons from Egypt.

The fairs were held outside, open to the elements, in the streets of the city. Goods were displayed in the rain, snow, sleet, and mud.

Francis probably spent as much time as his father allowed taking in the sights and sounds at the fair and in the town. This was a whole new world to Francis. The cities in France didn't resemble Italian cities. Instead of tall stone towers, these buildings were half-timbered, frequently with larger upper floors that hung precariously out over the streets. The rooflines were mansard, having two slopes instead of a single, even slope, and the building facades were more fanciful.

The city was a riot of color and festivity. Lords, courtiers, jesters, gentlemen, and ladies from the court wore a spectacle of fashion. The nights were consumed with drinking, dancing, and carousing. Of most interest to Francis, of course, were the entertainments. Troubadours sang; jugglers and acrobats performed feats of skill; knights tilted and crossed swords, while the minstrels and jongleurs enchanted the crowds of merchants by giving dramatic and tuneful recitals of the epics of chivalry.

Marie, Countess of Champagne, about a dozen years before Francis was born, commissioned a poet named Chrétien de Troyes to take the adventures of the Arthurian knights and put them to verse for the court. His stories became popular all over Europe.

One of Francis's greatest heroes, in fact, lived in the Chateau de Brienne just twenty-five miles from Troyes. His name was Gautier de Brienne. According to the stories Francis had heard, when Gautier's father was killed during the third crusade, he took his father's place on the battlefield and captured the city of Acre from the Saracens. His younger brother, John, was also regarded as a skilled fighter. It was John who would raise his sword at the age of seventy to stem a Saracen charge on the banks of the Nile and save the lives of thousands, including Francis himself.

3

THE PLAYBOY

To get back one's youth, one has merely to repeat one's follies," wrote Oscar Wilde. Francis engaged in many follies. He wasn't alone in them, of course. The indiscretions of youth seldom occur in isolation. Everything Francis and his friends did, they did together.

Holidays and festivals came frequently, allowing both young and old to spend hours in the piazza watching trained animals, jugglers, acrobats, and traveling players or listening to the troubadours. Francis himself became known for singing the songs of the troubadours as he walked down the street.

A market and meeting place by day, the *Piazza del Commune* was a place for entertainment in the evening. People met there to drink, gossip, and exchange news with pilgrims, travelers, and mercenaries. Whenever Pietro came home from his trips to France, it is likely he talked about his adventures in the world beyond the Alps. This was the equivalent of reading today's evening newspaper or surfing the Internet—the only way to know what was going on in the world beyond Assisi. The town crier was a source of some news, but his were mostly official announcements involving the city officials, court cases, or perhaps proclamations coming down from the Duke of Spoleto, under whose authority most of Umbria, including Assisi, functioned.

This kind of entertainment was far too tame for Francis and the youth of Assisi. Wild evenings of drinking, music, and dancing given by organized circles of the young were the thing to do in Tuscany and Umbria at the time. In summer, the curfew was relaxed so that the revelers could leave their courtyards and gardens to roam about the city. Francis threw himself into this kind of life with complete abandon, given over to singing and carousing with his friends, frequently drunk, roaming day and night through the streets and hangouts of Assisi.

Morality in the Middle Ages was an uncertain standard. Every December, for example, the town seemed to take a vacation from morality. A boy bishop was elected and robed in the church of San Nicolo on the saint's feast day. That was a prelude to a three-week bacchanal known as the December liberties. The churches were open to feasting and drinking, erotic singing, dancing, and the presentation of plays.

As seems to have been true in most eras, young men in Assisi dressed to be seen. Francis spent lavishly on opulent clothing and enjoyed parading down the streets wearing the latest fashions. A poor boy may have worn only a shirt and pants, but a wealthier youth wore a robe that dropped to just above the knee. Instead of pants he wore hose fitted with soles; a pocket-bag hung from his belt, and on his head was probably a kind of berretta made of red cloth.[1] Francis did have one strange quirk. At least once, he augmented the expensive material in his outfits with pieces of cheap cloth. Whether this was equivalent to buying jeans with built-in patches or some unconscious prelude to his later affection for "Lady Poverty" can only be food for thought.

All kinds of games were available. Those involving sleight of hand could be found on every corner. There were also public gaming houses Francis probably frequented to play a game of dice now and then. It was a popular pastime but known for provoking fights and even murder. Although losing was probably of little consequence to our wealthy hero, for others, who might be wagering all they had out of desperation, loss could mean ruin.

Thomas writes, "He was the admiration of all; and in pomp of vainglory he strove to surpass the rest in frolics, freaks, sallies of wit and idle talk, songs and soft and flowing attire." He also says that Francis "attracted many to join him in his frivolities," which means that he was not a mere participant but a leader. Francis threw around money as if it were confetti, surrounding himself with ostentatious splendor and a school of young men who were quite willing to partake in his generosity. He funded grand banquets noted for "their wantonness and buffoonery," according to Thomas. These were held in large halls, courtyards, loggias, or gardens, and also in the piazzas, where the tables were within a fenced-in area covered with tapestries and floral decorations. He would then be declared "master of revels," and given a staff to raise pompously as he strutted around.

When neighbors commented on her profligate son, Pica responded, some say with a touch of a prophetic spirit, "What do you think of my son? He will still be a son of God through grace."[2]

Pietro undoubtedly participated in similar raucous behavior

as a youth, but he reprimanded his son for his lavish spending, saying that he was acting more like some great prince than a mere merchant's son. Brother Leo, Francis's most constant companion throughout his later life, was the author of *The Legend of the Three Companions*, written around 1244. Leo combined his own memories of Francis with those of the previously introduced Angelo of Tancredi and another close friend of Francis named Rufino. Like Thomas's biographies, this work makes little attempt to maintain chronology, but it is very valuable as a firsthand account that intimately portrays moments in Francis's life. Leo writes that his parents "tolerated his excesses because they loved him and didn't want to upset him."[3]

Leo's use of a word meaning "upset" raises the question: Was Francis temperamental? Further testimony suggests otherwise, but he may well have been a rebellious teen in spite of the frequent use of corporal punishment.

This kind of behavior wasn't just a teen fling. It continued until Francis was nearly twenty-five years of age. If it seems strange that a man of twenty-five should continue to act like a wild teenager, we need to first understand that the independence of young men in those days had little to do with age. The adolescent stage for the elite in much of northern Italy was defined by social and economic dependence. A man was subject to his *patria podestas*—the father or head of the household—until he established a livelihood of his own. Since Francis, like many young men, was more or less apprenticed to his father, that period was prolonged.

He might have ended this dependence sooner if he had married. Men were usually married in their mid-twenties. Girls, on the other hand, would be married much younger, from fourteen to seventeen years of age. It must have seemed unfair that males should enjoy a long, leisurely period of adolescence and youth while girls had adulthood thrust upon them soon after puberty by early marriage, childbearing, and household responsibilities.

Marriage, in any case, was not an easy matter. Falling in love was not sufficient cause for marriage, nor was it required. As a rich merchant, Francis's father would need to seek a bride for his son whose class and wealth were basically equivalent to his own. A dowry was a critical element in any marriage between families of substantial means. The negotiations for the marriage contract could drag on for years.

Francis is recorded as talking about a bride several times. The subject, however, was usually brought up by his friends. Maybe they knew that the idea was on his mind; maybe they were poking a little fun at Francis for having a secret love or having none at all. There is never an indication of whether he had a specific lady in mind. Knights in his chivalric fantasies, after all, were never chained down to one woman.

Given the strong element of sensuality in every act at the banquets he attended, it is safe to conclude that Francis was no virgin. Women also attended the entertainments. It was apparently quite an honor to be invited, despite a city ordinance that forbade women to attend evening dinner parties outside their homes.[4] How much this law was flaunted is open to speculation. Most of the wealthiest women, the daughters of nobility, were generally guarded like prisoners, required to be accompanied by a nurse or responsible adult at all times. It seems likely that most of the women who joined in the evening festivities with these wild young men were not the finer young ladies of the city. They were women who had nothing dowry-wise to lose but who might hope for an advantageous arrangement with a well-to-do man.

Their desperation was well-founded as girls in poorer households were less desirable. The necessity of a dowry made them expensive to marry off and they were of no more use to their family after marriage. A boy, on the other hand, could be expected to continue working in the family business. Accumulated records suggest, in fact, that there were significantly more cases of infant death for girls than for boys.[5]

Poorer girls were therefore quickly on their own and subject to innumerable pitfalls. Aside from domestic servitude in wealthy households, few reputable occupations were available for single women. Finding a man to support them was crucial, but without a dowry the pickings were grim. They could all too easily find themselves trapped into becoming concubines or prostitutes. Amazingly, older women were the usual instigators, hoping to support themselves by pimping out the young girls. In one recorded case, a woman named Maria was said to have been a priest's concubine after which she became her daughter's pimp. The priest could not be held economically responsible for either Maria or their illegitimate daughter.[6] Given the limited choices, prostitution seemed a reasonable economic decision.

The situation was quite different for unmarried girls in noble and well-to-do households. Virginity was a lucrative bargaining chip in a marriage contract, sometimes worth a fortune; without her virginity a girl brought disgrace and dishonor to her family and herself and risked a discarded life. Virginity in a young man, on the other hand, was a social liability,[7] at least among one's peers, for sexual experience was a sign of masculinity, much as it is in many social circles today.

That, of course, doesn't mean that wealthy girls didn't cheat once in a while, as does Juliet, with the help of her nurse, in Shakespeare's *Romeo and Juliet*. A woman testifying at the canonization proceedings for Saint Clare of Assisi said that she accompanied teenaged Clare to clandestine meetings with a young man.[8]

There were, of course, more formal social occasions in Assisi, where some of the finer young ladies could make an appearance in the company of their families. From all reports, in spite of his excesses, Francis was a pleasant person to be around, generally kind and affable. One can imagine that he could frequently be heard laughing across a large hall, for he was light-hearted, rarely brusque, and, as Brother Leo writes, never "uttering a rude or offensive word to anyone." Many people in Assisi thought that he would indeed "someday be something great." Such gossip fed his ambition. He seemed to yearn for fame—to attain what his heroes had achieved—glory and honor and all the glitter that accompanied them.

Beyond the bawdy behavior, beyond the occasional acts of mischief in which any youth can become involved, was the rebel who didn't want to become a merchant—and an anger that drove him toward forbidden practices.

Thomas says that Francis was an "instigator of evil deeds." Admittedly, Thomas is given to hyperbole and moral sensationalism, but he goes on to write that Francis incited his friends to "crime."[9] It is difficult to know if he is referring to crimes in the legal or spiritual sense. A clergyman might be inclined to lump them all together. On the other end of the scale, the faithful often do not like to hear the name of a beloved saint connected with evil deeds.

The Assisiani were not a gentle folk. Feuding families were prevalent, as demonstrated by the many fortified houses. In fact, Assisi was rife with about as many rivalries as there were distinctions between people—between craft guilds, neighborhoods, social classes, occupations, and so on. They were willing to fight at the least provocation—arguing in the court and guildhalls, fighting in the gaming houses, rumbling in the streets—more often at war than at peace.

In Florence, and probably in Assisi, adolescents played a game called *battagliole*. The basic idea sounds familiar. Boys fought simulated battles using fists, wooden weapons, and stones. Youngsters, of course, play war games today, and Little League games sometimes lead to confrontations between surly dads, but in those days the game could get violently out of hand, eventually drawing much of the city into a bloody melee in which both adolescents and adults wielded knives, lead balls, and clubs against one another.[10] It is extremely doubtful that the youth of the city, who are by nature hormonally volatile, would be immune to the violence so prevalent in their society.

The group of young men Francis ran with had a name. They were called "The Sons of Babylon," and he was their leader. Generally where there is one group of young men acting under a banner name, there are others, creating a social scene where rivalries and resentments are bound to arise.

Shakespeare portrayed just such a violent Italian youth culture in his famous romantic tragedy *Romeo and Juliet*. The tragedy that came to the two unfortunate lovers was fomented when the rivalry between their two families was played out in the streets of Verona by youth gangs fighting with swords and knives.

It does not take much of a leap to envision Francis and his Sons of Babylon fighting with rival gangs in the streets of Assisi. However idealized the *chansons* may have been in their depiction of knighthood, the essential foundation of chivalry was war, and Francis had trained for years to be a warrior.

However endearing we may find the paintings of a gentle Francis singing to the birds, we must realize that human relationships in Assisi were volatile and often brutal. Fighting and warcraft could be said to have been indigenous to the people of Umbria, although that statement might seem presumptuous coming from someone writing in the wake of a century that featured two world wars, several acts of mass genocide, and at least three regimes that annihilated millions of their own citizens. Perhaps the violence in northern Italy could be considered more excusable for a people who had only recently emerged from one of the most horrific periods in human history: the Dark Ages.

THE KNIGHT OF ASSISI

The world Francis knew was like a sea of mountainous waves driven by winds of conflict. It had been that way beyond memory in the darkness that only old men could speak of. Civilizations had come and gone with hurricane fury, leaving death and devastation in their wake. Walls were erected and torn down in quick succession, and the number of those dying often far exceeded those born.

Rome had been the center of the empire for eight centuries when Emperor Constantine erected and consecrated a new capital in AD 330. Established on the site now occupied by the city of Istanbul, Constantinople was a grand metropolis, more central to the current boundaries of the empire, but the move left the city of Rome increasingly vulnerable to forces both north and south. During the centuries in which the Roman legions prevailed over much of the world, the city of Rome had become the golden apple among cities, the treasure house of the world, glowing with promises of great wealth to every civilization with strength of arms and an ambitious warlord. Invaders came one after the other with increasing daring until finally, in AD 410, the Visigoths drove south through Italy and sacked the city.

From a certain point of view, the centuries of carnage to which Umbria and much of Italy were subjected after the fall of Rome were due to an engineering triumph. In 220 BC, the Roman General Gaius Flaminius supervised the construction of the famous north/south corridor through Italy called the *Via Flaminia*. Built by the army, it extended from the city of Rome northward about two hundred miles through Umbria and on to Ravenna on the Adriatic. Paved with stone and sand, it vastly improved the ability of Rome to move men, arms, supplies, and trade goods into and out of conquered territories. Three years later, perhaps as a portent of the horrors that would eventually follow, Hannibal brought his Carthaginian army down that road to Lake Trasimene in Umbria and completely massacred the Roman army under Flaminius's command, including the general himself.

After the fall of Rome six hundred years later, this road became the primary route by which barbarian armies passed through Umbria on their way to Rome, each one leaving a ravaged, desolate people in its wake.

After the Visigoths came the Huns under Attila. The Vandals, who had already conquered much of northern Africa, sacked Rome in 455. The last Western emperor of Rome was deposed in 476 when the Goth Odoacer invaded and deposed the child emperor, Romulus Augustus.

The eastern emperor Zeno encouraged the Ostrogoths to regain Italy for him. They instead took Italy and made it a separate kingdom under their king Theodoric. A new eastern emperor, Justinian I, sent an army under his general Belisarius to recapture Italy, which was accomplished by 560.

One hundred years of Gothic wars had left Umbria in the grip of famine, its people reduced to eating dogs, rats, nettles, grass, or excrement and dying in the multitudes. With their magistrates executed and their cities burned to the ground, survivors fled into the hills and mountains. Stripped of their leaders, their fighting men had little strength to withstand the Lombards when they invaded eight years later. A Lombard kingdom was eventually established in the region that is still called Lombardy in Northern Italy. Over the succeeding two centuries, the Lombards expanded southward, gobbling up most of Italy until Pope Stephen II appealed to the Franks for help. They eventually defeated the Lombards and, on Christmas Day in the year 800, Charlemagne knelt before the high altar of St. Peter's in Rome to receive the imperial crown from Pope Leo III. Word spread across Europe that the Roman Empire had been revived, this time as a Holy Roman Empire.

With the death of Charlemagne, the empire again weakened and splintered. Power in Italy fragmented into the hands of the feudal lords—the territorial dukes and counts, most of them Lombards, who still dominated beneath the control of the Franks. Local feuds and local wars transformed law into anarchy.

Barbarian invasions resumed in the ninth century, exploiting the disunion of the Italian states. The Magyars flooded in from the north and the Saracens from the south.[1]

Finally, less than three generations before Francis was born, the people, subjected to centuries of cataclysm by the lords of fire and steel, began to forge a new society. In response to the terror of wandering hordes of Magyars and the ineffective defense by the feudal lords, the people began fortifying their cities and creating local militia. A patchwork of small city-states formed in Umbria and Tuscany, none of them strong enough to resist the power of the empire, but each managing to be nominally allied to church or empire while conducting its affairs largely independent of either. New houses and country castles rose up across the still rich quilt of Umbrian farmland. Roads were built, linking monasteries, castles, and villages as well as the major towns and cities. City walls were rebuilt and fortified.

In the minds of the people, though, warfare had become a constant. On the broader scale, this was the time of the crusades. Francis was five years old when Jerusalem fell in 1187. All of Christendom reeled from the shock, and a holy gloom spread out through the land, boiling into anger and a determination that drove new crusades. Francis was gripped, like everyone else, with an intense desire to drive out the infidel and free the Holy City. He could have imagined himself becoming, like the de Brienne brothers, a hero in the Holy Land, his horse rearing, banner waving, and sword slashing a path through the rushing horde.

On a smaller but no less violent scale, throughout northern Italy, neighboring cities engaged in persistent conflicts with one another: Venice against Genoa, Genoa against Pisa, Pisa against Lucca, Lodi against Milan, Faenza against Ravenna, Florence against Siena, and Assisi against Perugia.

Assisi and Perugia were near neighbors—only fifteen miles apart—within sight of each other on a clear day, but they had been at each other's throats since before Roman times, when Perugia was an Etruscan city across the river from the Umbrians.

As the cities and the communes grew in strength, a new conflict began to emerge, one that would have been thought impossible a hundred years earlier—class warfare.

Feudalism had been born in the warrior society, which arose following the collapse of the empire. Warlords paid their warriors for military service with land. These warrior nobles, however, were not farmers but professional soldiers who could be called up for battle at any time by their lord. To produce wealth, they needed workers to till the land. Unable to purchase arms and traumatized by generations of devastation, disease, and starvation, common people were all too willing to work the land and pay, with their produce, for the right to live under the protection of the lord.

This system made each person answerable to another in a hierarchy that extended from the most destitute peasant all the way up to the king or, at the time of Francis, to the Holy Roman Emperor. The organization of society was therefore very simple but also very rigid. The way people at the time defined it, "There were those who pray (churchmen), those who fight (the nobility) and those who till the earth."[2] As much as Pietro and the other merchants may have resented it, they were technically among the *minores*—the lowest class—as was, of course, Francis.

A celebration called *Calendimaggion*, held in the springtime, pitted the *maiores* of Assisi in mock warfare against the *minores*. It was a major event that drew people from neighboring towns to join in the fun. The combatants used blunted arms, but the fighting was fierce, tinged with resentments and class hatred. Many were wounded and some even killed before one side or the other would concede defeat and end the game.[3]

The broader rivalry between the *maiores* and the *minores*, however, only grew more intense. From the look of the landscape around Assisi, feudalism was in full flower. Castles were on every hill, in every valley, near rivers, and above precipices—all over Mount Subasio.

A strong visual image of this class structure can be seen in Assisi itself, as Adrian House, one of Francis's more recent biographers, describes in detail. At the top of the feudal order was the emperor, whose sometime residence, the sprawling fortress *La Rocca Maggiore*, loomed high up on Mount Subasio.

Below *La Rocca*, or "The Rock," was San Rufino. There, on the northern edge of the city, around the piazza of San Rufino, was the exclusive part of the city, called *la sopra*. This was the abode of the nobility, who were often descendants of the various fighting forces who had invaded Umbria—Lombards, Franks, Germans, and so forth. Many of them, because of their love of fine clothing and elegant cloth furnishings, visited the establishment of Pietro di Bernadone, on the next level down.

Called *il sotto*, it was the level of the market and the Piazza del Commune, the city's economic and political center. The streets below the piazza were the workplaces of craftsmen, merchants, manufacturers, and shop keepers. Further down were manufacturing houses outfitted with kilns, forges and ovens, slaughterhouses, stables, and chicken houses.[4] The lowest level, down by the wall on the edge of the marshes, was occupied by dilapidated houses, lean-to shacks, and broken-down warehouses, where lived the original *minores*—the lowest elements of society.

While the clergy and nobles remained the dominant class, craftsmen, merchants, physicians, and lawyers were growing in number. These citizens came together to discuss things like the building of roads and bridges, passing legislation, minting currency, dispensing justice, and contracting alliances, with little or no consultation with emperor or pope.

To merchants, though, nobles in their castles were predatory beasts who swooped down on them when they happened to pass along a road overlooked by their citadels, demanding payment of a toll for the right of passage. The nobles, as the ruling class, also had the right to implement forced labor, increasingly looked upon as a form of slavery. As the merchant class increased in strength, their resentment of the nobles grew stronger, as did their desire to free themselves from feudal tyranny.

Twenty years before Francis was born, Assisi had been captured by the Emperor Frederick I, called Barbarossa, in 1160. We have no details of what happened except a few notations that suggest great horror. The emperor was well aware of what was happening in the cities. Otto of Freising, one of his supporters, wrote: "There is not a powerful man anywhere who does not obey the laws of the city; and the city, while expanding in every way its authority over the neighboring territory, does not shrink from conferring knightly dignity itself on young men of inferior condition."[5]

The city dwellers had had enough of kings and emperors and feudal lords. Some supported the church, which had been growing as a political rival to the emperor. Only fourteen years after the imposition of imperial power, in 1174, the citizens of Assisi rose up against the imperial forces but were defeated.[6]

Henry VI, the emperor during Francis's youth, often stayed in that huge castle, *La Rocca*, on the mountain above the city.

When the emperor was not there, the citadel was generally occupied by Conrad, Duke of Spoleto, the emperor's nephew. When Francis was about thirteen, the emperor entrusted his wife and newborn son, Frederick, to Conrad in La Rocca.

Most of the city, including Francis, turned out to watch the celebration that accompanied the christening of the baby who would become Frederick II. The spectacle included a colorful procession of armed knights down the road from the castle with a grand entourage of guards, their banners waving, marching to the sound of trumpets and the beating of drums. Although conflicts between church and state were at their height, a strong presence of prelates and clergy was there representing the church as the future emperor was baptized in the same font as Francis had been thirteen years earlier.

This pomp and ceremony, however, did not salve the hatred that the people of Assisi felt toward the Duke of Spoleto, his garrison up in La Rocca, and the nobles who supported him and the emperor. That same year the emperor had stepped up pressure on the cities and every other belligerent to submit to his authority. Some of those who stood against him were sawed in two; others were crowned with crowns of red hot iron. Gregorovius writes that "the savage slaughter was carried on in a frenzy of blood and torture."[7]

Two years after Frederick's christening, the death of Emperor Henry VI, in 1197, provided the vacuum that enabled class conflict to finally erupt.

In the aftermath of the emperor's death, Pope Innocent II requested Conrad to surrender his domains and allegiance to papal control. Conrad accepted, but in 1198, while he was away from La Rocca to take care of legal requirements for the change, Assisi's merchant class revolted and laid siege to the fortress.

Francis, who was fifteen or sixteen at the time, probably took part in the siege. It was said that they pulled down The Rock "stone by stone." They used these stones later to reinforce the city walls and build defensive towers.

The revolt against the landed aristocracy resulted in massive destruction. One by one each castle was put under siege by the commune. Sasso Rossa, the castle that guarded the road from Assisi to Spoleto, was left in ruins. Monaldo di Offreduccio had extensive lands and many castles about the area, but he was driven from all of them. And as each noble house in the country fell, their town houses were ransacked and burned as well.

One noble family, who fled just before their house next to the Cathedral of San Rufino was razed, included a bright-eyed five-year-old girl named Clare, who would one day play a very important role in Francis's life.

Most of the displaced noble families, including Clare's, set up households in Perugia. There they waited, simmering in hatred for Assisi's commune, and looking toward the day when they could return and wreak vengeance on the rebellious Assisiani.

Occasional skirmishes followed, with each side making forays into enemy territory. Assisi continued to reinforce its walls and towers with stones from the castle, and Francis continued to refine his fighting skills. At about the time he turned twenty, rumors from Perugia suggested that the anger of the disenfranchised knights of Assisi was about to boil over. The always hostile citizens of Perugia would welcome any excuse to raise arms against their bitterest enemy. In truth, Assisi was no match for Perugia, which was more than twice as large and much richer. The magistrates of Assisi sent out calls for alliances and mercenaries to join them and prepared for war. The time was ripe for twenty-year-old Francis to prove his mettle for knighthood.

Assisi took the offensive, hoping perhaps to find the warriors of Perugia unprepared; Assisi's warriors assembled on the piazza of the cathedral. The clopping of nervous horse hooves on the cobblestones was already stirring up fragmented emotions as the heralds raised their long, slender trumpets for the fanfare. As the trumpet blasts echoed through the twisted corridors of stone, the drums began to beat, driving the frenzy for battle still higher in the assembly of warriors. Their weapons and armor reflected the sunlight in tiny bursts all across the crowd of anxious wives, children, and parents. None shone more than those of Francis. He probably wore a hauberk, or metal tunic, of chain above leggings also made of chain, providing him protection from head to ankle. A surcoat, worn over the chain mail, was painted with his colors or family arms. He would have worn a steel helmet with a metal nosepiece jutting down from the headpiece.[8]

The procession began and Francis rode along with the knights southwest down the street toward the city center. Soon they passed people standing between the columns of the Temple of Minerva, and then the cheering crowd gathered in the Piazza del Commune. Francis would have waved to his mother fearfully watching through an upper window of the house on the south side of the street. Continuing down the Via Portico, the long procession finally passed through the city's main gate. An ancient structure, built by the Romans, the Porta Sant'Antimo towered nearly three stories above the train of soldiers. Outside the gate they passed the great wooden carriage of Assisi, which held an altar and a crucifix. Drawn by a team of white oxen and draped with the red and blue colors of Assisi, it was brought out only on special occasions. Standing beside the carriage was the Bishop of Assisi, giving them his blessing.

Perugia was known for brazen ruthlessness in battle. Their emblem, appropriately enough, was a clawed and snarling griffin.

The advancing forces of Assisi were within about three miles of Perugia when they turned off the road and climbed a hill toward a hamlet named Collestrada, forming a line between a church and a small castle. They could see Perugia down the road; behind them, still within view beneath the evening shadow of Mount Subasio, was Assisi. If he followed protocol, Francis put on the pair of long heavy gloves called gauntlets and adjusted his lance and shield, checking the position of his sword and mace hanging at his side.

Soon the forces of Perugia emerged from the city and approached the battleground. What eventually ensued was called the Battle of Collestrada. With the Assisi force on the high ground, the Perugians recklessly charged up the hill into a hail of arrows. Francis was packed in very close beside the other mounted warriors, lances raised. This minimized the usual defense against a cavalry charge, which was to unseat the knights by killing their horses.

Assisi repulsed the first assaults, but, for unexplained reasons, lost command of the high ground. The momentum of the fighting shifted against them. Amid shouts, the clash of steel against steel, the cries of pain, and the groans of the dying became more numerous until those were the only sounds. It had turned into a massacre. The only lives the Perugians spared were those for whom they could expect a good ransom. Francis was one of those taken prisoner, possibly because his rich armor made him appear of noble birth.

The prisoners were herded through the streets of Perugia, while lines of jeering crowds pelted them with vegetables or mud or worse. There they were placed in a dungeon that had been constructed within the city's Etruscan foundations. It was cold, dark, damp, and stinking with decayed food, urine, and the accumulated remains of feces. The prisoners could be expected to be kept alive but nothing more.

Perugia had a particularly gruesome reputation with regard to their treatment of captives. They were known to have shod captives like mules or to have stuffed their mouths with toads. Sometimes they even wrapped them in straw and set them on fire or otherwise tortured them as entertainment. We are not told if Francis was subjected to torture.

Amazingly, the spoiled and petted playboy Francis seemed to handle imprisonment better than most. In fact, his disappointed and grumbling fellow prisoners resented his upbeat attitude. Perhaps he tried to sing some of the troubadour songs or tell them some of his favorite stories. In a darker moment he might have bragged, as he often had before, about the greatness that lay before him. He did say, "for I will yet be venerated throughout the whole world."[9] Upon being told of this statement, Thomas of Celano interpreted it as being prophetic of the sainthood Francis would eventually achieve. Whatever it was, the other prisoners took it as the rambling of a madman.

Francis kept no journal of his reactions to the harrowing experiences of 1202, but hell might have seemed less gruesome than the chaotic spectacle of friends and acquaintances being hacked to death, every memory of their vibrant lives reduced in an instant to butchered flesh. Added to this were the screams of foes impaled upon his sword and the haunting image of light abandoning the eyes of those slain before his face. Francis was not one to leave his dreams and experiences unexamined. Brutal reality had come crashing down on his fantasies of chivalric fame and glory with consequences that would only slowly be played out.

We get snippets of his character while confined in that merciless dungeon—fragments of who he had been and perhaps the man he was becoming. One of the prisoners was ostracized because he had injured one of the others during the battle. Francis took it upon himself to work out a reconciliation. He tried to help another man as well—one who was being shunned by the others for being "a proud and completely unbearable knight." We can only conjecture, but, given the circumstances, he might have been one of those who tended to complain incessantly, blaming others for his misfortune. Whatever the case, Francis was patient with him and treated him kindly until his attitude became more palatable.

One of the few happier experiences for Francis in prison was provided by a knight from Apulia, a region southeast of Rome. He told Francis stories of his exploits with Francis's hero, Gautier de Brienne. In particular he described a battle that had occurred in June 1201 in which Gautier had led a phalanx of only a few hundred French knights in assaulting an imperial army of five thousand in Capua and won.[10]

There were others among his fellow prisoners with whom he formed lasting relationships—some who would play significant roles in his future life. Federico Spadalunga was a cloth dealer of noble heritage from the city of Gubbio, not far from Assisi. He would prove to be a true friend when all others abandoned Francis during his conversion. Giovanni di Simone, a young landowner, was also there. He would be present on the night that Francis died and attest to seeing an amazing sight that would quake the entire Christian world.

Another nobleman—one of those who had remained in Assisi and fought for the city—was Angelo di Tancredi, the son of a distinguished consul, who might have helped Francis learn his fighting skills. Their time together in prison may have furthered their friendship, planting the seed of faith that would eventually prompt him to join Francis in his order. He would, in fact, become one of Francis's closest friends and one of the three responsible for *The Legend of the Three Companions*.

Francis remained in prison for nearly a year before negotiations for the return of the prisoners reached an agreement. By then the squalid conditions had taken their toll on his health. He returned home gravely ill.

5

FROM RICHES TO RAGS

F rancis fought through the winter of 1203 against the grasp of death. Since he was still pale and emaciated by the following spring, some scholars say it was malaria or tuberculosis that imperiled his life. Francis recovered enough to occasionally get up and limp around the upper story of the house. Through his window, he could watch people mill about the market. Beyond were the burned-out remains of dark towers cluttering the once tranquil skyline. Farther left and higher up the mountain was the pillaged carcass of the once proud *La Rocca*.

Thomas believed that God brought sickness upon him "so that the pain might take his sense away from wanton thoughts and give him time to think about other things."[1] More interestingly, he goes on to say that God looked down and "removed his [Francis's] fury from him." What exactly that fury was is never elucidated. Was his anger directed toward the vicious cruelty and butchery the city of Perugia had inflicted upon him and his fellow Assisiani? Was it directed more generally upon the corrupted nature of unredeemed mankind who could commit such atrocities on his fellow man? Or had his idealized vision of chivalric knights been so tarnished that he felt betrayed by the deception?

There was also the possibility that his anger emanated from a far older and deeper source of conflict. Fathers, as we have seen, had much greater power—legal control, in fact—over their sons in those days than they do in our age, and Pietro had a reputation for being a hard man—ruthless and threatening. Francis's playboy behavior, as well as his overblown fantasy for knighthood, was a source of irritation to his father. It is not surprising that much of the man he became and the way of life he chose were diametrically opposed to everything his father represented.

That year in the dungeon, trying to survive under the most depraved conditions, must also have been daunting to this pampered boy, especially as he felt disease drawing him closer to death. Under those circumstances, it would have been natural for him to turn to God, praying for deliverance but believing his prayers to be hampered by his former dissolute life.

The ravages of war weren't all that he saw from his window. In the spring the grassland at the top of the mountain was covered with wildflowers, orchids, and pheasant's eye narcissus. Forests of ilex, oak, and pine were clustered tightly around the periphery. And, if his tower window was high enough, he could look back to his far right and see the dell spreading out from the base of the mountain, quilted with fields, farms, vineyards, and olive groves.[2]

So much beauty on every side and yet he was "not moved" by it. Thomas says that he began to think that "people who enjoyed the beauties of the fields and vineyards were fools" and "began to despise himself for having loved such things and began to hold those things in contempt."[3]

This seems to be a strange attitude for a man who is recognized today for his love of nature. He might simply have been depressed, of course, but Thomas suggests that these thoughts reflected a broader transformation: he was beginning to withdraw from the world. The object of his disdain was not nature itself, but all things that are valued by the world of people.

While Francis was wrestling with issues personal and spiritual, Assisi was mourning its dead and the consequences of defeat. Perugia and Assisi chose two arbiters who, in November 1203, drew up what they called a "Peace Paper," although it largely represented the demands of the formerly disenfranchised Assisiani nobility. It began, "Because there is in Assisi discord between the [nobility] and the men of the people over the destruction of the castles and feudal servitude . . ." It went on to list the names of the offended feudal lords and to order that the commune of Assisi construct new houses and towers for them.[4]

Amid the sounds of hammers and chisels and wagons lumbering under the weight of stone quarried from the mountain, Francis tried to return to "normal" life in Assisi. It was not an easy transformation. During the last days of his rehabilitation, he was described as being unsettled, agitated, depressed, or sometimes hyperactive. Whatever had begun in Francis, though, was incomplete. Unsure of what to do, he tried to resume his old life. His friends, probably missing his generous contribution to their revels, were anxious to have him back feasting and drinking and carousing with them.

Resuming his old life also meant returning to his work and

to the rigors of becoming a merchant. We do not know how much of his wealth Pietro had sacrificed to ransom his son, but he was seemingly patient enough to allow Francis a long period of rehabilitation. He may have thought that after such a devastating clash with the brutal realities of life, Francis would now dispense with his foolish fantasies and youthful excesses and settle into a merchant's life.

Less than a year after returning to work, however, Francis jumped at the chance to revive his hopes for knighthood. Glory, honor, and money were the objectives an Assisi nobleman ascribed to his knightly venture. The motivations was Apulia, a region maybe a week's ride southeast to the boot heel of Italy. It was an opportunity Francis could hardly ignore, for the expedition was to join up with knights under the command of Gautier de Brienne. Gautier had given the call to arms to reclaim the region for the Normans, whose sovereignty had been usurped by German overlords. Here was the opportunity Francis had long dreamed of—to receive knighthood at the feet of his long-time hero.

Francis purchased the most expensive clothing and equipment he could find, much more than a merchant's son could normally afford, once more, no doubt, setting his father's head spinning. He may not have been a knight, but he was going to look like one.

He had proved himself under the most rigorous of circumstances. He was ready. But then Francis had a vision, probably while he was home sleeping the night before his departure. The people of his day paid great attention to dreams, as if they were a direct conduit between heaven and earth. In his vision, Francis saw a "beautiful palace occupied by a beautiful bride." It was very elegant and filled with shining knightly armor and weapons.

Francis asked whose palace it was. A voice spoke to him, telling him that it "belonged to Francis and his knights."[5] The next day, as he was wandering about Assisi gathering supplies, his great happiness was apparently displayed on his face, prompting people to ask why he was so happy. He answered, "I know that I will become a great prince."

Thomas says that the ambition driving him, however, did not go unchallenged. He writes that Francis "had to do some violence to himself to carry out the journey." Whatever the word translated "violence" here means, Francis experienced some kind of fierce inner struggle. Another pattern of thinking had been growing inside Francis—some other motivation for living that no longer fit within his former schema of attaining fame and glory. Was it the prospect of fighting and killing that troubled him, or was it the worldly ambition he was submitting to? As we have seen, warfare was an integral part of life in the twelfth and now the thirteenth century, and Francis never donned the mantle of a pacifist.[6]

He did do something completely out of step with his ambitions a day or two before the company was due to depart. Both Leo and Thomas write that he gave all the refined clothing that he had acquired to a poor and nearly naked knight. Perhaps Francis remembered how Saint George had given away his horse and armor to the poor after slaying the dragon.

Whatever his state of mind, Francis was dressed and anxious to leave when he joined the company of knights in the piazza of San Rufino late in 1204. The air billowed with the white breath of men and horses in the cold morning air as the bishop blessed them and made the sign of the cross over them. The people delighted in any opportunity for spectacle, and the city gathered to witness the departure of knights for battle. Even the girl Clare, the enigmatic figure always in the background of Francis's life, now about to become a teenager, may have watched Francis in the ceremony from her tower window overlooking the piazza.

The group—nine in all, warriors and yeomen—marched through the city, presumably in a procession like the one taken by the warriors of Assisi for the ill-fated battle with Perugia. But today their destination was Spoleto, about twenty-four miles to the south. The company of nine was to join up there with the regional militia for the journey to Apulia.

But as they rode along the Flaminian Way and came within sight of Spoleto's unfinished cathedral tower, Francis began to feel ill—perhaps a recurrence of his former illness. He fell behind the others, nursing his discomfort, and then, amid the silence in the wake of the departed mounted company, Francis heard someone speaking to him. Still on horseback, Francis may have spun about looking for the source. But there was none, just a voice moving on the wind. It asked him where he wanted to go. Francis explained in halting phrases his plan to go to Apulia— his hopes of serving under the great Gautier de Brienne.

But then the voice asked, "Who can do more good for you, the lord or the servant?"

The answer seemed obvious. "The lord, of course," Francis said.

"Then why are you abandoning the lord for the servant, the patron for the client?" the voice replied.

Francis puzzled over this quietly. *Was not Gautier a lord?* He suddenly realized the truth. "Lord, what do you want me to do?"

The voice said, "Go back to the place of your birth, for through me your vision will have a spiritual fulfillment." He thought of the vision that had given him so much joy—the palace, the shining arms, the bride. It had seemed so clear when he first saw it, but the voice told him that he needed to understand it in another way.

His thoughts stirred by what he had been told, Francis couldn't sleep that night. *It was a palace for me and my knights.* That's what he had been told in the vision. *What else could it mean?* The lonely ride back to Assisi along that ancient road gave Francis time and solitude to consider what was happening to him. He had always wanted to be a knight, and the vision had offered knighthood and a palace.

Perhaps he stopped to drink from the Spring of Clitunno, sacred to the Romans, where the legions stopped on their way to meet Hannibal and his Carthaginian army. It was such a tranquil, lush setting; he might have rested there and sifted through his thoughts and prayed. Maybe then is when he made the decision mentioned by Leo: "Changed in mind, he now refused to go to Apulia and desired to conform completely to the divine will."[7]

People must have cast questioning looks as Francis rode through the streets of Assisi without the companions he had left with in such glory the day before. Local gossip may have brought up the possibility that he was a coward for turning back. No mention is made by his early biographers of such a reaction, although some people did ask if he was still going on to Apulia. Such questions would be stifled in six months or so, when news reached the city of the battlefield death of Gautier de Brienne. In June of 1205, he and his troops were ambushed near Apulia and massacred.[8]

A clearer indication that Francis suffered little or no public embarrassment is that he was again drawn into the wild social life of his friends. Naturally, since he had been their leader, the Sons of Babylon again wanted him to organize one of their wild and lavish banquets. Francis had always been the obvious choice for them because of his wealth and generosity and, of course, his willingness to pay their expenses.

He did what they asked, as he had so often done in the past. Thomas says that Francis didn't want to spurn his old friends because he didn't want to be thought "avaricious," withholding money for himself. This may have been how he looked upon his father, who was known to be tight-fisted in his business dealings. Generosity was a code of chivalry as well as a Christian virtue.

When he was walking home after the revelry one night, still holding the ornate staff traditionally held by the "Master of Revels," he watched his friends singing drunkenly, passing beneath arches and tripping down ranges of steps, vomiting out all his expensive food. Was that how he wanted to live? Were they who he wanted to be? He felt out of place and began to fall behind. Leo writes that he was "overcome with a sense of such tenderness from the Lord that he could not speak or move."

When his friends looked back and saw him lagging behind, they stumbled back to him and asked if he was thinking about taking a wife. Maybe the look on his face resembled the look of a man in love, or maybe they were just asking in jest. Francis got his tongue back and answered, perhaps with a laugh as well,

"You are right! I was thinking about taking a wife—one more noble, wealthier, and more beautiful than you have ever seen!" The trio of men behind *The Legend of the Three Companions*— the men who knew him best—write that he was thinking about the "beautiful bride *poverty*" who may also have been the bride in his earlier vision of the palace.[9]

His friends moved on with laughter and drunken singing, provoking the inhabitants of the houses along the street to shout, in protest, from their windows. Francis let them go and slipped off another way, discarding the staff and singing the songs and psalms he had heard in church all his life. He might have sung softly at first, mostly to himself, and then with more abandon as the fervor driven by that speechless moment grew within him.

Who was this wife who was "more noble, wealthier, and more beautiful than" any other? If she was "poverty" as Leo maintains, Francis was seeing poverty in a totally new light, not as most people view poverty—not even as those do who feel deep compassion for the poor.

It was easy to become poor in those days. A bad harvest, an illness, a broken leg, the death of a husband or a father, failure to pay back a loan, a house fire, or a bad roll of the dice was all it took and a person could end up begging to survive. There were few safeguards in the social and economic system—no insurance policies or food stamps—to aid people in trouble, and a significant percentage of the population led a subsistence lifestyle. Beggars were a familiar sight in Assisi, as were the unapproachable lepers who had to announce their presence by shaking a rattle. The former were everywhere, begging outside the churches, in the piazzas, going door to door, and stumbling along dusty roads.

But Francis may have developed a more intimate connection with poverty through his father's business. The Bernadone family's wealth in cloth manufacturing and merchandising was largely built upon the labor of underpaid people—the *minores*—who lived in the most impoverished areas of Assisi down against the lower city wall. Pietro likely called upon Francis occasionally to make a trip near the mosquito-infested areas to retrieve a missing piece of cloth or to check on a missing worker.

Whereas the Roman engineers who built Assisi had provided for the care of sewage on the upper levels, down there, especially in wet weather, the streets were open sewers. In winter it was damp and cold, the flimsy and fragmented walls offering little insulation from the icy winds. In the summer these shoddy environs baked with heat and were infested with fleas, mosquitoes, and lice.

Francis would have had to leap over puddles contaminated by waste, dodge garbage suddenly thrown from a sagging doorway, and enter a home that was no more than a drafty lean-to, all the while frantically swatting away flies. Along the way he might see packs of rats running between tenements and hovels. It was also the breeding place for any number of communicable and often deadly diseases—tuberculosis, smallpox, leprosy, definitely dysentery, and sometimes even malaria and typhoid.

Francis was not indifferent toward the poor even during his wasteful youth. One day when he was busy selling cloth in his father's shop, a poor man came in begging alms "for the love of God." Francis ignored him but later regretted it, thinking that he would probably have responded better if some lord had come in. Francis decided that if he was courteous and generous to the wealthy, he should be that way with the poor as well. He decided from that point on never to turn down a person who asked in the name of the Lord.

Now, though, he began to be even more generous to the poor, determined never to let one go away without some gift. If he had no money, he would give a hat or a belt. If he lacked those he would give the shirt off his back. He bought items for the adorning of churches, sending them particularly to the poorer priests. Leo wrote that when Francis's father was out of town, Francis would set a lavish table of food for just him and his mother (Perhaps his brother Angelo was now traveling with his father?) so that he would have extra food to give to the poor later.

Some scholars suggest that, during this period, Francis may have come under the influence of a movement called *Ordo Penitentium* or "the penitential order."[10] So far, however, they had failed to gain the favor of the church leaders.

There were, in fact, several groups who espoused a life of poverty. Some had been declared heretical, their members made fair prey for mistreatment or even death in some locales.

Whether or not Francis explored the ideas of any of those movements, he was entertaining thoughts that were new and unique to him. Instead of fantasizing about knighthood, Francis began to wonder what it would be like to live in poverty. He thought about going to a distant city where he would exchange his clothing for the rags of a poor man and even go about begging.[11] Clearly his interest in poverty went beyond just a concern for the poor, however important that was.

Francis soon got his wish. He decided to take a pilgrimage to Rome. Being the center of Christendom, Rome was a frequent objective for pilgrims, offering not only the great churches and the Holy See but also the holy relics of Peter and Paul.

Early in 1206 Francis left for Rome. He wore a pilgrim's cloak and cap he had gotten from a poor person and carried with him only a staff and a sack containing hard bread and wine. It was a three-to-four day walk from Assisi to Rome. For purposes of safety, pilgrims traveled in groups, staying in monasteries and hospices along the way. No one wanted to be on the road after dark, when thieves and wild animals might find them easy prey, so one hospice was rarely more than a day's travel from the previous one. They lived very simply, using their cloaks as blankets and their staffs as walking aids, although a staff could also prove an effective weapon if bandits approached.

Francis saw the wall of the great city long before he reached the gate. The glory of Rome had long ago been shattered by repeated invasions. Instead of buildings wrapped in majestic colonnades, tall monuments, and grand arches, hundreds of dark, fortified tower houses now dominated the skyline. Coming down the Flaminian Way, Francis and his companions crossed the Tiber and finally entered the ancient metropolis through the Porta Flaminia. The city opened up before them, half jungle and mostly in ruin. With no officials to watch over them, the monuments had decayed, aided by flooding from the river, the building of tower houses (sometimes atop ancient homes), and increasing accumulations of rubbish that buried the ancient city ever deeper into its primordial soil.

According to Ferdinand Gregorovius, who wrote a multi-volume work entitled *History of the City of Rome in the Middle Ages*, Rome "resembled a huge field encircled with moss covered walls with tracts of wild and cultivated land from which rose gloomy towers or castles, basilicas and convents crumbling to decay."

Its colossal monuments were wrapped in vines and its baths broken, while its aqueducts, temple colonnades, and triumphal arches were surmounted by towers within "a labyrinth of narrow streets interrupted by rubbish heaps. . . . The yellow Tiber, passing under broken stone bridges, flowed sadly through the ruinous waste . . . Vineyards and vegetable gardens lay scattered like oases through the whole of Rome . . . baths and circuses were overgrown with grass" and often stood in marshlands. "Everywhere that the eye rested," there were "gloomy, defiant, battlemented towers built out of the monuments of the ancients."[12]

Three streets converged just inside the gate. Francis's route lay along the one that angled to the right. After passing by the Pantheon he took a sharp right turn and walked another quarter mile to the Vatican bridge. There, with the cylindrical castle of San Angelo across the river to his right, he again crossed the Tiber. St. Peter's was only a short distance away at the foot of Vatican Hill. The basilica that Francis gazed upon was not the one now in Rome. This one had been built by Constantine in 330 over Peter's grave. It was huge—the largest basilica in the city, one-third larger than the Lateran, which was the official cathedral of Rome.

There was no paved piazza in front of the church then, just rough ground teeming with pilgrims, priests, and other clergymen being preyed upon by peddlers hawking souvenirs and relics of questionable authenticity. If Francis wasn't in such a hurry to enter the church, he might have stopped at one of the carts scattered about the area and purchased some refreshments.

A broad range of steps led up to an arcade through which he passed to enter the vestibule. Beyond was a large rectangular atrium surrounded by arcades. Francis hurried through the open middle of the atrium, passed the large fountain, and walked through another arcade to enter the church. His first glance down the nave must have brought him with a gasp to a sudden stop. Shafts of light shot through the high clerestory windows at a sharp angle, illuminating a vast space. The building was more than 400 feet long with a nave proportionally as broad. High above was a trussed timber roof whose peak may have risen as high as 125 feet above the floor. The overall impression was of a building on the scale of the Astrodome.

Francis finally caught his breath and started the long walk through clusters of clergy, pilgrims, and sightseers toward the altar. Two much smaller aisles ran on each side of the nave, or central aisle. These five aisles were separated from each other by arcades, each composed of twenty-two columns. The walls that bounded the outside aisles were decorated with frescoes, which people, mostly visitors, admired as they walked leisurely along the wall. The people on the inner aisles moved more quickly, more interested in getting from place to place than in sightseeing. People in the nave did both since the entablature—the high walls on either side of the nave—were decorated with magnificent frescoes.

A brilliant mosaic dominated the vault of the apse he was approaching at the west end, but his eyes focused on the baldachino, a large canopy set above the saint's tomb at the crossing of the nave and the transept.[13]

Looking down at the tomb, Francis could see coins scattered around, but considering the number of people strolling about the church, he was troubled that there was so little given in remembrance of Saint Peter. This was his church, after all, and what could be more amazing than viewing the tomb of this giant among men? Francis, therefore, made an extravagant offering. His coins splashed on the tomb like a rain of hail, made even more impressive as it echoed through the great arched vaults. The gasps and cries of startled people resounded in answer, their eyes wide and fixed on the little man in the pilgrim's cloak.

He then strode back through the hallowed, cavernous nave toward the portico. There Francis got his much anticipated chance to experience what it was like to be a beggar. A large number of poor were situated in the vestibule and on the steps before the church. He asked one incredulous beggar if he could trade clothes with him. Then he, the son of the richest man in Assisi, sat happily among the poor on the steps of the church for the rest of the day, begging—in French.[14]

6

A NEW LIGHT

No one ever begged with so much abandon as Francis did that day on the steps of St. Peter's. The fact that he was begging in French meant that he was excited and happy. Nearby beggars must have thought Francis to be very strange indeed. Poverty obviously attracted him, but for reasons that were not immediately apparent.

His emotions were wide open, but his thoughts were a disorganized tangle and he didn't yet know where they were leading him. After returning to Assisi, Francis again turned to God and began to withdraw daily to pray. Leo says that he began to think of himself as "having little value" and began to "despise" the things he had formerly valued.[1]

Here again is a pattern of thought that is alien to most of the modern world. Such thoughts do not mean that he was having a bout with depression. In fact, rather than depression, he was feeling a profound happiness. He told others that, as he prayed, he found a "sense of tenderness" visiting him time and again. He was experiencing a total reorientation of his entire system of values, one in which his personal comforts, pleasures, and desires were no longer supreme but subservient to something, not yet quite definable, that was of far greater importance. He kept remembering the story told by Christ about a man who sold everything he had to buy a "pearl of great price." Francis believed that there was something—not a physical object but something non-corporeal, spiritual in nature—of such value that one would give up everything to obtain it.

At one point his prayers took a dark turn. Leo writes that he began to be troubled "by the devil." He was given an evil vision of a horribly hunchbacked woman often seen haunting the streets of Assisi. He was going to become like her, the devil taunted him, if he did not turn from the way he was going. Francis was terrified, but he soon realized that the dream was only a temptation.

One day while he was fervently praying, he received some kind of a word telling him that he had to learn to despise everything that he had once "loved carnally" if he wanted to learn God's will. At the same time, he was told that what he had once despised would now be "sweet and delightful."[2]

We rarely hear the word *carnal* these days. *Carnal* refers to one's physical needs or appetites, especially as contrasted with spiritual or intellectual values. It is most often used in reference to pleasures offered by sex, food, popularity, and ostentation. Pleasure is a powerful motivator. Despising things that offer pleasure takes considerable self-control and determination. Learning to love what he had formerly despised, as Francis was soon to discover, required a relaxation of those controls subject to long-held prejudices.

Francis had always felt an aversion to lepers. Thomas says

that if he saw a leper walking along a road or sitting atop some distant vantage, Francis covered his face. Even when he was moved to give alms to a leper, he turned away his face and held his nose.

Soon after receiving the message about things despised, he was riding along a road near Assisi when, practically on cue, he encountered a leper. He swallowed hard, his usual sense of disgust and maybe a little nausea beginning to rise. We can imagine that he pulled up his horse sharply, letting it turn about and paw the ground restlessly through his moment of indecision.

The word *leprosy* in the Middle Ages tended to include a number of other diseases that caused disfigurement, including syphilis, gonorrhea, and St. Anthony's fire. Even true leprosy is only mildly communicable, requiring prolonged physical contact to be passed on, but the horror and fear of it provoked extreme measures. To protect the inhabitants of cities and towns in Italy, lepers were forced to live outside of the city in what were called "lazar houses," named for the biblical leper Lazarus. There were several lazar houses near Assisi.

Becoming afflicted with leprosy was one of the great tragedies of the age. Upon entering a hospice, lepers were required to bow before an altar while a priest led them in making a solemn vow. In spite of the severity of its pronouncements, it did reveal a level of compassion toward these unfortunate people:

"Dear poor little man of good God, by means of great sadness and tribulation of sickness, of leprosy, and of many other miseries, one gains the kingdom of heaven where there is no sickness or sorrow and all is pure and white, without stain, more brilliant than the sun. You will go there," the priest continued, "if it pleases God. In the meantime, be a good Christian; bear with patience this adversity and God will be merciful to you."

The vow offers additional comfort: "My brother, the separation has to do only with your body. As for the spirit, which is more important, you are still as you were before, a participant in the prayers of our Holy Mother Church. Charitable men will provide for your lesser needs and God will never abandon you. Take care of yourself and have patience. God is with you. Amen."

The priest then sprinkled dirt over the leper's head and said, "Die to the world; be born again in God." Then he prayed above him, "O Jesus my Redeemer, who made me of earth and clothed me with a body, make me to rise again in the new day."

The final instructions pretty much describe the lifestyle of a leper:

"In the name of the Father, the Son, and the Holy Spirit, my brother, take this cloak and put it on as a sign of humility and never leave here without it.

"Take this flask. Put in it what will be given you to drink, and under penalty of disobedience I forbid you to drink from the rivers, from the springs, from the wells.

"Take these gloves. You are forbidden to touch anything with your bare hands that is not yours.

"If, while walking about, should you meet someone who wishes to talk to you, I forbid you to reply before you put yourself against the wind.

"You are forbidden to be with any woman who is not of your family. You are forbidden to touch young people or to offer them anything; and from eating from anything but your own leper's bowl; and from entering churches or rectories, and from going to fairs, to mills, and to markets; and from walking through narrow streets where those who meet you cannot avoid you.

"Take this tentennella [rattle]; carry it always with you. Sound it to warn others of your presence."[3]

Francis swallowed his horror, dismounted, and approached the leper. There were penalties for disobeying the directives stated above, so the leper was probably waving his rattle frantically as this strange and foolish young man approached him. Then, to both his surprise and horror, Francis suddenly reached out, took the leper's hands, and kissed them, an action that would have been considered incomprehensible. Francis then gave the man a few coins and returned to his horse. When he turned his mount about, the leper was gone. Maybe the leper was an angel sent by God to test Francis. Perhaps the leper had been so amazed and terrified by this encounter that he ran off in a combination of joy and hysteria.

Francis considered this to be the most significant moment in his conversion. He opened his *Testament*, written not long before his death: "The Lord gave to me, Brother Francis, thus to begin to do penance; for when I was in sin it seemed to me very bitter to see lepers, and the Lord Himself led me amongst them and I showed mercy to them. And when I left them, that which had seemed to me bitter was changed for me into sweetness of body and soul."[4]

Francis was not content with one symbolic moment. A few days later, he went to a hospice for lepers and, while distributing money to them, kissed the hands of each. He continued to associate and zealously minister to lepers throughout the rest of his life, washing away all "foulness" from them and cleansing their wounds. He instructed his followers to do the same and even to seek shelter among lepers when they were traveling.

After this monumental breakthrough, Francis continued to pray in solitude, on occasion neglecting the work in his father's shop to seek the presence of Christ. He must have felt that caring for lepers was not the primary thing God wanted him to do, for he prayed that God would give him direction and teach him to do his will.

Francis turned to a person referred to as his "best friend" and confidante, an unnamed person who accompanied him to out-of-the-way places, into the nooks and crannies in and around Assisi, and, in particular, to a cave on Mount Subasio. Wherever they went, they would talk about "things" and about what Francis called a "great and precious treasure." This friend was even willing to wait outside the cave while Francis went inside to pray, "eager" to hear more about this treasure when Francis came back out.[5] There were many caves all over the region. In the years to come, as Francis traveled around, he was especially alert to places where he could pray in solitude. He eventually accumulated knowledge of many such places, creating a circuit of hermitages all over Umbria.

The identity of this best friend is never disclosed. One might think that such a friend—someone Francis trusted with his most intimate thoughts—would have been an early convert to his way of life. Bernard and Peter of Catania, his first named followers, were businessmen. Of the three men who would later be identified as the "three companions," Leo was a priest and Angelo a knight; neither was likely, any more than were Bernard and Peter, to be found following another young man around as if they were two adolescents keeping a secret from the rest of their playmates. Rufino was younger and a little shy, but that kind of intimacy isn't seen in descriptions of his dealings with Francis. The question remains: if this person was indeed his first follower, why didn't he join with Francis immediately?

There is a sense throughout his extended conversion that Francis was in some kind of chrysalis stage, experiencing the pain of breaking out into a new kind of creature. Even the tenor of his prayers began to change. Thomas said that he was going through "great travail" in his spirit as thoughts flew into his mind in quick succession, so much so that it troubled him. The sins in his former dissolute life weighed heavily upon him.

He began to fast frequently and to an extreme, ever more fervently seeking. What was it he was seeking—truth? The nature of God, the presence of God? He may not have known for certain himself, except that he wanted to understand who he was and what he was to do with his life.

Despite moments of "travail," Francis left almost every encounter with God filled with an indescribable happiness. It bubbled from him like a mountain stream, and he couldn't hold it back. People in the streets could see it in his face—the wide-eyed expression, eyes bright, as if he "glowed with a Divine fire." Day by day, like successive rays of light breaking through a cloud, the revelations came and he drew closer to the understanding he so desperately sought. Thomas writes that one day "the Lord showed him what he must do." The specifics are not elucidated, but it was a breakthrough that made him even more ecstatic with happiness than before, so thrilled that be began to talk "carelessly" about his revelations to his old friends.

Whatever Francis said, it made no sense to them. Knowing of his obsession with knighthood and his desire to perform great deeds, they asked if he was going to Apulia to become a knight. He responded that he was not going to Apulia but that, instead, he was going "to do great and noble deeds in his native place." There was still something of the knight left in him, but he now saw his service as belonging to another lord. Francis was becoming, as Leo described it, the "knight of Christ!"[6]

Thomas, in his *Second Life*, says that sometime later, Francis was walking by a little "wayside church," now mostly in ruins, hedged between a forest of olive trees and the ruins of a Roman sepulcher. He was somehow moved to go inside and pray. The church, named San Damiano, had a low vault and a narrow window—a mere slit like those used in fortresses through which defenders shoot arrows. The church apse was semicircular and painted blue with a field of stars. He fell down before an old painted crucifix that was dangling above the altar. While he was praying before that image, the painted form of the crucified Christ on the crucifix suddenly moved its lips.

Then Francis heard words spoken "tenderly" by those painted lips: "Francis, don't you see that my house is being destroyed? Go and repair my house, which, as you see, is falling completely into ruin."

Thomas says that Francis was almost "deranged" by the incident, his connection with reality deeply shaken. Perhaps thinking that no one would believe him, he apparently told no one about "this strange visitation" at the time.

Francis took the words of the crucifix very literally. He went to his father's shop, picked up a bolt of expensive scarlet cloth, along with some other items, and then rode off to Foligno, a small city known for the production of paper, about a fifteen minute ride if he rode at a gallop. There he sold everything, including his horse. With money in hand he then walked back to San Damiano. This time he found a poor priest there. He kissed his hand and offered him the money.

The priest, however, didn't trust Francis. He had seen Francis parading about the city and knew him to be a profligate youth who was the leader of a band of reckless and mischievous young men. He therefore suspected that Francis was playing one of their heartless tricks on him and refused to take his money.

Francis tried to convince him of his sincerity, finally asking if he could just spend the night there with the priest in San Damiano. The priest finally gave in to the latter request, though probably with a degree of distrust. He still refused to accept the money, however. That decision was due, not to Francis's reputation, but to his father's. The young Bernadone boy may no longer have been living down to his reputation, but the elder Bernadone, Pietro, was not one he was prepared to tangle with in a temper. Francis shrugged and cast the money onto the sill of that narrow window as if it were nothing and paid no more attention to it.

Whether Pietro first noticed the missing cloth or his absent son, he was soon scouring the town looking for Francis. During his search he began running into people who told strange stories about his son. To Pietro it sounded like Francis was out of his mind or going through another of his wild and crazy phases. Why he had heard nothing of his son's behavior earlier— the hours spent in prayer, his bizarre behavior in town—is a mystery. He was, of course, a busy man. But now hearing these things, Thomas says that he was both "grieved and enraged."

Francis was betraying his trust and bringing shame on the family name. Eventually someone told him that Francis was living at the broken down church of San Damiano, so he rounded up his friends and neighbors and set out to retrieve his son. Why he needed a large delegation to accomplish this is not clear. Perhaps he thought that the Sons of Babylon were holed up there with Francis.

The sound of these people approaching, either on foot or horseback, must have resembled the approach of a band of vigilantes or a hanging party. Francis was well acquainted with his father's temper, so he scrambled into a kind of a dark "pit" or "cave" beneath the church. Thomas says that Francis had prepared this hiding place ahead of time, apparently expecting his father to respond just as he did. There he listened to the loud voices and trampling feet above, praying fervently that the Lord would protect him from persecution—in this case, from his father.[7]

THE CHRYSALIS BREAKS

A shaft of morning light peeking through the ragged break in the floor above must have been a welcome sight every morning. Oil for lamps was expensive, so Francis spent much of the time in the dark. That crack in the floor was the only entrance to this ancient, crumbling subterranean chamber.

The hidden chamber beneath the small church was not a Christian place. The few symbols crudely inscribed on the walls were of another religion—one of the many remnants of the pagan world that was once the Roman Empire. It had been a place where soldiers passing through might stop to offer worship and sacrifices to the goddess Mitre.[1]

The local priest may have known about the chamber and used the area to store foodstuffs like flour, grain, and wine, and maybe as a hiding place for the more precious pieces of church hardware and other materials—crosses, cups, chalices, and vestments. The musty smell of decaying plants and insects, along with the more acrid odor of mildew, probably dominated the atmosphere.

Considering the poverty of the church, probably no more than a flimsy ladder made of small tree branches roped together provided entry to or, if needed, escape from this place. Francis remained hiding in that dark womb in the earth for a month, eating food that was brought to him secretly.

For that entire month Francis prayed almost continuously, wrestling with his thoughts and emotions. Thomas says that he spent that month seeking "to possess wisdom which is better than gold and to get prudence which is more precious than silver." It is questionable, however, given the outcome, that the objectives of his prayers were that clearly defined.

We are never told who smuggled food and other necessities to him during that month, except that it was the one person "in his house" who knew about his hiding place.[2] Most likely it was his mother, who often stood between Francis and his father. Some scholars suggest, however, that the smuggler of food and supplies was the same "friend" and confidante mentioned earlier.[3]

An hour spent praying is a long time for most people. Praying for an entire month suggests that Francis was agonizing over his new direction—trying to attach meaning to his experiences and explain what he was all about in the eyes of God. He knew that he was effectively leaving everyone and everything he had ever known. No matter how much he had tried to explain it to his "friends" and people on the streets of Assisi, no one, except perhaps his secret friend, seemed to understand this great treasure he had discovered. Standing alone is rarely an enviable position. Outsiders have always been regarded with suspicion—easy prey for mockery, disdain, and persecution.

By the end of that month Francis had begun to feel glad

about his condition.[4] That sounds like a logical determination, but what is happening here is much more profound. It is his final, resounding victory over doubt, the tearing open of the chrysalis—the moment of rebirth. Francis crawled out of the earthen darkness a new creature—the new man whom people would someday call a saint.

Leo writes that God filled him "with an inexpressible happiness and enlightened him with a marvelous light."[5] Glowing with this inner radiance, he left the church and stumbled up the road toward Assisi, prepared to face his past, to risk rejection and persecution from his friends, his family—from so many of the people he had known all his life.

We are now back to where we began his story—at the moment Francis feared the most, when he shed the trappings of his previous life to accept the new. Seeing his emaciated body and his strange behavior, seeing him praising God as he walked along the street with his hands held high, the people saw such a change in the man they had known, a behavior so different from the usual, that they took the joy in his demeanor as madness.

The riot of persecution we pictured earlier continued for some time. Then his father, whose shop was right on the main street, heard about how Francis was acting and being treated. *People were making fun of his son!* Embarrassed and filled with fury he went out into the city. Leo says that he "ran like a wolf after a lamb." Then there, in the middle of the public melee, he picked up his son and carried him back to his home.

Still filled with rage, Pietro shoved Francis into a very dark room—perhaps a basement—and locked him in as if he were a prisoner. Shortly thereafter he went into the room/prison and argued with him heatedly. When that failed to work, he whipped him and locked him in chains, certain that he was right to turn his son away from his madness and folly.

Finally, Pietro had to leave on business. Still boiling, he left Francis locked up and in chains. After Pietro was gone, his mother, who hadn't liked how her husband was treating Francis, began to talk gently with her boy. Maybe she recalled for him the stories of the knights—their manners and courtesy—their honor. Perhaps she brought up instances from his childhood—good times they had enjoyed together. She may have even tried to convince him that his mad behavior was not proper for a good Christian.

But when Francis proved determined to continue in his new way, she freed him from his chains. After his treatment earlier, we might have expected that he would retreat back to San Damiano, but instead he went back among those who had abused him earlier and roamed about trying to tell the people his wonderful discoveries concerning Christ.

When Pietro returned and found that his wife had released Francis, his fury again burned and he beat her before once again rushing back into the city looking for his son. He planned to run Francis out of town so that he would no longer be an embarrassment to the family. But when he got to his son this time, Francis stood up to him, saying that he would "undergo any evil for the name of Christ."[6]

Francis eventually returned to San Damiano to undertake the task that he understood the painted lips had told him to do—to rebuild that church. Such a task was not undoable for the former dandy, since he probably had taken part in dismantling La

Rocca and in building the new wall around Assisi. Francis used the receipts from his sale of the horse and the cloth to secure supplies for building the church as well as to help the poor.

Francis's father, however, was not finished dealing with his rebellious son. He decided to put the matter to the court, so he stormed in before the city magistrates and demanded that they get back the money his son had *stolen* from him.

Francis spurned the request, however, saying that he would not come since "he had been made free by God's grace." It is a profound irony that, however much the life Francis espoused was in diametric opposition to the current practices of the clergy, he retained a conviction that the church was still the body of Christ. He therefore did not hesitate to align himself with it and to seek its protection. The fact that he had effectively obtained sanctuary in the church meant that he was no longer subject to the secular court. The magistrates consented that he was right and told his father that there was nothing they could do.

Pietro, on the other hand, had not accumulated his wealth by giving up easily. Since Francis had chosen to shield himself behind the church, Pietro was going to seek legal restitution through the church. He therefore went to Bishop Guido of Assisi, intending to formally renounce his son and demand that he give back everything he owed to his father.

The bishop dutifully summoned Francis. This time Francis had no choice but to appear and he responded, "I will appear before the lord bishop, because he is the father and lord of souls."[7]

The trial before the bishop took place on a cold morning in March of 1207. The bishop's palace, still standing today, was built into the walls of the city and looked more like a fortress than a place dedicated to spiritual affairs. It was located not far from San Giorgio where Francis had attended school. From the palace courtyard, Francis would have been able to see his temporary home and workplace, San Damiano, in the valley below.

The trial did not take place in the courtyard where the bishop normally held such proceedings, which is how Giotto portrayed the scene in his fresco. The winter that year is recorded as having unusually heavy snowfalls, so the ground would have been covered with snow. The bishop therefore opted to hold the trial in the great hall of his palace.[8]

Typically a crowd of spectators would be in attendance, from priests and lawyers to beggars and petitioners, most of them waiting for judgments regarding their specific cases.

There may, of course, have been others present—Francis's mother and her friends, maybe even his former friends and, perhaps, some of his former enemies as well.

The bishop was aware that Francis had been using his money to do good works—rebuilding San Damiano and helping the poor—so sometime before the proceedings, he took Francis aside and counseled him to return the money, saying that "he should not use what was gotten unlawfully to do good works."[9]

Consequently, when the official proceedings began and before anyone else said a word to him, Francis walked from the hall into another room, took off all his clothes, laid the money on top of the pile, and then returned naked before his father, the bishop, and those standing nearby. He gave the clothes and money to his father, saying, "From now on I can freely say 'Our Father who art in heaven,' not father Pietro di Bernadone, to whom, behold, I give up, not only the money, but all my clothes too."

The bishop was deeply moved by the young man's fervor and recognized that Francis "bore a great mystery," so he gathered him into his arms and covered his nakedness with his own mantle. From then on, Thomas writes, the bishop became devoted to Francis, helping him, encouraging him, and loving him.

When Pietro left with the clothes and money, he was denied a sense of triumph, for the spectators were indignant that a father would leave no clothing for his son to wear and had pity on the young man.

What followed must have happened very quickly. The bishop gave Francis a rough peasant's tunic with a chalk cross drawn on the back. Perhaps he would have given him something more substantial, considering the cold weather, but Francis ran off into the woods in an excited state. His flight eventually took him to Gubbio, about twenty miles away, so some people have concluded that Gubbio was his destination from the moment he left the trial. But why would any rational man be going all the way to Gubbio on foot in the cold of winter wearing nothing but a slight tunic? He did eventually receive another tunic in Gubbio from an old friend, but he could probably have gone back to San Damiano in a very short time and achieved the same result.

Thomas writes that he ran away from the bishop's palace scantily clothed and plunged into the woods, singing praises to God. We can imagine him bounding through snow drifts and leaping carelessly over obstacles along the path, too overwhelmed with emotion to notice the cold.

Along the way he was accosted by robbers who asked him who he was. His answer was hardly appropriate for a man in such a dangerous situation. He responded, "I am a herald of the great King. What is that to you?" This, of course, was total nonsense to the robbers, so they beat him and threw him into a pit filled with snow. As they walked away, they jeered at him, calling him "a clownish herald."[10]

Francis made no decision to go to Gubbio. He didn't know or care where he was going. He could have ended up anywhere in his ecstatic state.

He had realized something after his impromptu but dramatic ceremony in the bishop's hall. *He was free!* His fear of his father, his destiny as a merchant, his desires for popularity and fame, his need to impress others—he had conquered them all and found a new life in which Christ was his devoted Lord and companion. He was ecstatic with joy.

Even his brutish encounter with the robbers didn't faze Francis. He just scrambled out of the pit and went merrily on his way, singing and praising God. If Francis did have a destination in mind when he bolted out of the bishop's palace, it would have most likely been the monastery he approached about two hours later. It was a Benedictine monastery in a town called Valfabbrica, along the bank of the river Chiagio. If his goal had been Gubbio, then he'd have been seeking shelter in the monastery just for the night. But he ended up spending several days with the monks.

Francis had no idea that he would one day found an order within the Catholic Church. He may have felt that monks, who had already accepted a life devoid of personal pleasures, would be most likely to understand his new devotion to poverty. For all he knew, withdrawing from the world and becoming a monk might have been what God had in mind for him. He could always go back and complete the task of rebuilding San Damiano. Other servants of Christ would surely understand the necessity of his fulfilling God's command. He was still singing praises when he knocked on the monastery door.

His treatment at the monastery, however, quelled his joy. Instead of welcoming him as a fellow servant of Christ, they summarily sent him off to work as a kitchen scullion, ignoring his hunger—even refusing him a drop of soup. In addition, although he was cold and hungry and wearing only a thin, short, and frayed tunic, no one offered him a stitch of clothing. One writer suggests that the Chiagio River was rising at the time and that the monks' concern for stemming the flooding waters was the cause of their inattention to Francis.[11] However it is unlikely that Francis would have overlooked such an emergency and not given allowance for it. A few days later, his experience at the monastery proving a major disappointment, Francis left, making his way another two hours' walk to what was then the nearest city, Gubbio.

In one of the city's fortified houses near the southern gate lived a friend named Federico Spadalunga (called "Frederick Long-sword"), a man Francis had fought beside at the battle of Collestrada and with whom he was imprisoned in the dungeon of Perugia. Francis remembered that this man lived in Gubbio and found his home. Theirs was a pleasant reunion, although Frederick was probably alarmed to see Francis so wan and thin and so plainly and unseasonably dressed. He did not hesitate to give Francis a more functional tunic that he could wear on top of his shirt for warmth. No doubt Francis tried to tell his friend about the wonderful things God had been teaching him. There is no record, however, of Federico ever becoming one of Francis's followers.

This headlong rush through the countryside, including his disappointment at the monastery, had given Francis's thoughts time to coalesce. Through the dramatic act of giving everything he had to his father, Francis had fully embraced poverty, both figuratively and practically. This in itself had given Francis an intoxicating sense of liberation. He not only didn't have anything, he was free of the desire to have anything!

It is a concept that few people can understand, because living for most of us has always been driven by the desire to acquire whatever might satisfy, not just our needs, but our desires. Francis was not rejecting the need for food, clothing, etc.—the basic necessities required to sustain life—but the drive to accumulate possessions. He saw what most people see only in brief flashes—perhaps after collapsing onto the couch after a hard day's work or at the moment the alarm buzzes in the morning—that such a preoccupation can be a form of slavery.

Francis, of course, went beyond secular considerations. From the very vivid example provided by his own life, he believed that our headlong pursuit of "things" tragically deprives us of the most precious possession of all—the presence of God!

That presence had become the source of the greatest joy Francis had ever known. In that presence he had found feelings of tenderness, profound enlightenment, and elation. That presence, he now believed, was the "pearl of great price"—the "treasure" he had talked about with his friend. But the only way to obtain that treasure was to give up every other "carnal" desire—to follow a treasure map traversable only through poverty. "Lady Poverty" may have been adorned in rags, but she was the lady of the palace of God.

8

RAGTAG BROTHERS

Francis returned to Assisi. He might have been free, but he was also alone. Both friends and family had abandoned him, with the possible exception of his mother, and most of the other people he knew thought him to be crazy. No further mention is made by Thomas or Leo of his mysterious "friend." Had he abandoned Francis as well?

To many, such a situation would be cause for despair. Francis, however, knew that he was not alone. His Lord was only a moment away, a constant companion of whose love he was assured and in whom he placed his trust. Without questioning the future, Francis set about the task assigned to him by God—to rebuild the little church of San Damiano.

Many of the stones used in the original structure were broken or shattered or had been purloined by people to build their own homes. Consequently Francis had to collect more stones. Apparently he needed more substantial stones than those he could collect around the countryside, so he went into Assisi in search of stones. Leo says that he offered people a reward for every stone.[1] Although he must have had little money, he paid them something, for we know of one man who later complained that he had been underpaid for his stones.

Some of the citizens of Assisi became used to seeing Francis going through Assisi praising God—"intoxicated with divine love," as Leo put it. Others pitied him for falling from such a lavish lifestyle to such a lowly state, while still more continued to think that he was mad. Surely no sane person would choose to live in poverty, they probably thought. Francis was learning to ignore their scorn.

The priest at San Damiano began to notice that, accustomed to the fine foods of the wealthy, Francis was having difficulty eating more common foods, now the only form of sustenance available to him. Although the priest himself was quite poor, he tried once in a while to bring Francis pricier delicacies. Francis accepted them gratefully at first but then began to realize that priests were not likely to be as generous to him everywhere he went. What was even worse, if he continued to want fine foods, he might end up going back to the life he had left behind. He then asked the priest to stop bringing him such refined food and began going about Assisi with a bowl in his hand, begging for scraps. Begging turned out to be worse than he expected. He was revolted by the scraps in his bowl and had to keep reminding himself of his calling before he eventually taught himself to be content with such food.

Pietro was pained and ashamed to see his son going about begging, so he began cursing his son whenever he saw him. Francis endured it for a while but then decided to take more overt action. He found a poor man and, in exchange for a portion of the alms Francis gained, convinced him to follow Francis about town pretending to be his father. Now, when Pietro walked by and cursed him, Francis would turn to the poor man and say, "Bless me, Father." His companion would then make the sign of the cross over Francis and bless him. After that Francis would turn to his abusive father and say, in an attempt to shame him, "Don't you believe that God can give me a father to bless me against your curses?"[2]

His biological brother, Angelo, also mocked him. One winter day, when his brother passed by, Francis overheard him say to his companion sarcastically, "You might tell Francis to sell you a penny's worth of his sweat." Francis responded, "I will sell that sweat to my Lord at a high price." Onlookers were impressed with the way Francis handled abuse and began to admire him.

Most of his time, of course, he spent back at the church making repairs and rebuilding the walls. Visibility was limited inside the church, especially when Francis worked late into the evening, so he liked to have a lamp burning. Unable to buy the necessary oil, he would go into the city begging for it. One day he came to a house in front of which several men were playing a game. Francis felt ashamed for them to see him begging; consequently, he turned away and slunk back down the street. But then he thought how foolish he was to still be concerned about the approval of others. He turned back around and determinedly walked back to the house. There he openly confessed his fault to the surprised group of men. Then, filled with a kind of "spiritual intoxication," as Thomas describes it, he went to the door, begged for oil in French, and received it.[3]

At one point during his reconstruction of the church,

Francis began crying out to those passing by that someday this church would become a monastery for ladies and that it would be renowned throughout the church. Six years later San Damiano would indeed become a holy place for the Order of Poor Ladies. Clare, the young girl mentioned earlier, saw him doing this and described it in her Testament written shortly before her death. You can almost hear her laughing as she writes, "Climbing the wall of that church, he shouted in French to some poor people who were standing nearby, 'Come and help me in the work on the monastery of San Damiano, because there will as yet be ladies here who will glorify our heavenly Father.'"[4]

While rebuilding the church, Francis attended mass at Santa Maria degli Angeli, a small church across the valley about two miles outside the city. There, on February 24, 1208, Saint Matthias's Day, which commemorates the apostle chosen to replace Judas, Francis listened to the priest as he read from Matthew 10. This is the passage where Jesus spoke to the apostles before sending them about to spread the news that "the kingdom of heaven is at hand." Included in his instructions to them is the following: "Do not take along any gold or silver or copper in your belts; take no bag for the journey, or extra tunic, or sandals or a staff; for the worker is worth his keep" (Matt. 10:9–10). Those words struck Francis, so he later asked the priest to clarify what the passage meant. After he digested what the priest told him, Francis said excitedly, "That is what I want to do!"

Until now Francis had been wearing the habit of a hermit, including shoes on his feet, a leather belt around his waist, and a staff in his hand. After hearing the words of Jesus, he decided to follow his instructions to the letter; he took off his second garment and threw away his walking stick, belt, and shoes. He then made a very cheap, plain tunic and tied a rope around his waist. His definition of poverty was now made more specific and had the seal of the divine word of Jesus.

After finishing his work on San Damiano, Francis walked all about the region surrounding Assisi, helping lepers. Then he moved on to repairing San Pietro della Spina, a dilapidated, nearly destroyed chapel near one of his father's farms. As he took on the work of repairing this church, he continued to pray, making confessions, doing penance, and regularly attending mass at Santa Maria degli Angeli. That church, close to the road from Foligno to Perugia, eventually became his third building project. It was more popularly referred to as *Portiuncula*, or "little Portion," the name given to the small section of land that it occupied.

The abbey of San Benedetto, located up on the side of Mount Subasio, formally owned Portiuncula, but the little church was generally abandoned except for the times when the monks would come down from the monastery to hold mass. It was a pleasant little spot within a wood of oaks and ilexes that also included a stream and some marshland, but it tended to be humid year round, sometimes foggy in winter and stuffy in summer.[5] Little did anyone know what an amazing destiny lay ahead for that little church, nor, for that matter, what the future held for this lonely "Knight of Christ."

Francis also continued to talk to the people of Assisi in the streets and piazzas and near the churches. He had a "treasure" to share with them—something of great value—but he couldn't seem to make them understand. Francis didn't have just an idea to share with them; he offered a relationship, which was as much a matter of emotion as of thought. Francis was linked to his Savior in a bond of love, which lifted him to the heights of emotion. Most people who walked the streets of Assisi had no way of relating to these highs. The world was a scary place and people knew that they needed God. But to intimately love God, that was strange, maybe even a little mad, especially given the outlandish actions Francis frequently displayed.

Sometime during that year after his conversion, Francis learned to moderate his flights of ecstasy and began to preach. He started at the same place where he had learned to read as a child—outside the church of San Giorgio. On any preaching occasion, Francis began by greeting the people with a proclamation of peace: "May the Lord give you peace!" As it turned out, Francis could be quite a speaker when he organized his thoughts. Many people in Assisi, including some of those who had formerly scorned him, now began to regard him with amazement. Thomas says that he preached repentance to all with simple words, but it struck his listeners like a "blazing fire" in their hearts.

Two years after his conversion, his preaching at San Giorgio drew the attention of Bernard di Quintavalle, a rich and highly respected notary and a land owner in Assisi. Bernard held degrees in civil and canon law, and many of the leaders in Assisi's government frequently solicited his advice. Apparently Francis and Bernard had been acquaintances at some time. Thomas says that Bernard "had often been hospitable to Francis and knew the kind of man he was."

Bernard came to Francis, though, in secret. He said that he wanted "to join him in life and garb."[6] He invited Francis to his home, where they talked late into the night. Bernard offered

Francis the opportunity to spend the night and they finally retired. Bernard was still uncertain about what he should do. One does not lightly dispense with as much wealth as he had to embrace poverty with only the promise of some mystical connection to God. He knew as well as anybody that the world had no shortage of fools and charlatans. Apparently his mental quandary was making it difficult for him to sleep, so he got up and began pacing about the house. As he passed the room where Francis was staying, he heard the fledgling preacher praying. It was very late—or early—and Bernard was convinced only a man sincere in his beliefs would devote such time to prayer.

The next morning, on April 16, 1208, Bernard asked Francis to tell him what he must do with his wealth. It appears that Francis wasn't sure at first if he should ask Bernard to do as he had done and give away everything he owned. Consequently Bernard and Francis thought it best to consult someone who was a man of the law. They chose Peter of Catania, who lived near the cathedral among the other nobility. Their discussion must have been very provocative, for when it was over Peter decided to join them.[7]

Although issues regarding the law had been satisfactorily addressed, they still hadn't determined what should be done with their possessions. They decided to submit that concern to God, so all three men went to the church of San Nicolo, next to Francis's former home, just across the Piazza del Commune. There they prayed for a while and then Francis randomly opened the book of gospel readings that was lying on the altar. The first passage he opened to read, "If you want to be perfect, go, sell your possessions and give to the poor, and you will have treasure in heaven.

Then come, follow me" (Matt. 19:21). Francis randomly opened the gospel again and read the passage he had found so provocative once before—the one in which Jesus tells his disciples to "take nothing for the journey—no staff, no bag, no bread, no money, no extra tunic" (Luke 9:3). Francis opened to another passage and read, "If anyone would come after me, he must deny himself and take up his cross and follow me" (Matt. 16:24).

The harmony among those three passages convinced Bernard to sell everything he had and to give the proceeds to the poor rather than to members of his own family. That was probably not a popular decision with his family, but his actions became the pattern for the admission of all future followers.

Thomas says that Francis had a "devoted follower" even before Bernard, but his name is not supplied. Perhaps he was that mysterious "friend" who accompanied Francis to the cave during the period of his conversion. Various speculations have been proffered in an attempt to identity these two people, but none of the early writings reveal their true identify. Whether or not the two are the same person, why did this follower not identify himself? Was he now ashamed to be seen with a man whom others considered to be mad?

Unfortunately, Francis and his two new brothers had no place to stay. They had no money and owned nothing. That, of course, was how Francis wanted it, but it did present a problem now and then. They finally went to the church that Francis had last rebuilt—Saint Mary of the Portiuncula. Thomas says that he finished building it three years after his conversion. Francis may have been staying there anyway after he finished his work. They didn't stay in the church, however. Nearby they built a little hut—very makeshift and of no value—to which they returned from time to time.

In spite of the moderate acceptance Francis had gained from his preaching, there was, at first, much hostility to the "brothers." Their early efforts to beg were a complete disaster. People mocked them, accusing them of disposing of their possessions so that they could live off others, which, unfortunately, sounds on the surface like a very reasonable complaint. Girls and women were frightened by their uncouth appearance, and both rich and poor alike laughed at these formerly wealthy men now scrounging about like dogs.

There were other kinds of complaints as well. After seeing how Bernard and Peter had given away all of their possessions, a priest named Sylvester confronted Francis with the accusation that he had been underpaid for the stones he had sold Francis earlier. Francis responded by simply dropping a handful of coins into his hands. Afterward Sylvester was ashamed of himself and, in not too many months, would appear at Portiuncula and apologize to Francis for his carnal behavior.

Sylvester would also tell Francis and the brothers that a few nights after he had acted so despicably, he had been given a strange dream in which he saw an immense cross reaching high into the sky. The foot of the cross was planted in the mouth of Francis, while the arms of the cross were spread out across the world.[8] After telling them of his dream, he asked if he could join the group. At the time he was, by far, the oldest member of the group and also the only priest.

Another man had been intrigued when he witnessed the great sell-off by Bernard and Peter. Giles had come to Assisi to take part in the Feast of San Giorgio, the patron saint of Francis's boyhood school. Like Francis, Giles had wanted to become a knight. Since the festivities honoring Saint George included a joust, Giles hoped for an opportunity to show off his knightly attributes. We do not know how well he performed in the joust, but what he had seen of the three brothers began to weigh upon him. Finally he left Assisi to find them and discover why three wealthy, intelligent men would give up everything they had and take up a life of poverty.

At the time the three brothers were apparently staying at Rivo Torto, a small shack on one of Francis's father's properties. Giles became completely lost on his way and was wandering aimlessly along country roads until he ran into them, purely by chance, near one of the lazar houses. They must have had an interesting discussion, the two aspiring knights. It is not clear whether Giles asked to join the brothers or if Francis invited him after he gave him this test: while they were talking, a poor man came by asking for alms. Francis immediately turned to Giles and told him to "give the poor brother your mantle." Immediately he did so, and Francis accepted him into their fellowship.

Now having three brothers all interested in the "life" he had begun alone, Francis started teaching them how to live in poverty and simplicity. Fairly soon, he decided to send them out to spread their message as Jesus had sent out his apostles. They were to take with them little more than the clothes on their back and no money at all. He divided them into two pairs.

According to the three companions, Francis was not yet fully preaching when he and Giles went to the Marches of Ancona on their first missionary journey. From the way their efforts are described, Francis seems to have been doing most of the talking—encouraging people to do penance. In the meantime, Brother Giles, who had a little bit of a comic flair, would flitter around, waving people toward Francis and saying things the equivalent of, "Hey, listen. He is really giving you the 'best advice.'" Apparently their enthusiasm was so ecstatic that some of the people became convinced that they were both mad. Others thought that only fools would say such things. Young ladies ran far away from them, trembling with fears of "being carried away by their foolishness and madness." It was not exactly the reaction they had hoped for.

A few days after they returned from their first foray beyond the environs of Assisi, three more men from the city, Sabbatino, Morico, and John de Capella, came down to Portiuncula, where they were now staying, and joined them. Sabbatino would accompany Francis to Egypt eleven years later; Morico was a Cruciger Knight, which meant that he fought with an order of knights who wore the emblem of an orb topped with a cross, symbolizing Christ's dominion over the world. Francis nursed Morico through a long illness while he was working in one of the leper houses. The third member of the team, John de Capella, on the other hand, would one day fall astray. A few days later, one more brother joined them. He was Filippo (Philip) di Lungo from an area on the eastern slope of Mount Subasio called Costa di San Savino.[9] He was a very tall man, so they dubbed him "Philip the Long."

The apparent failure of the brothers to move people to penance must have weighed heavily upon Francis, and his prayers probably included requests for direction. One day, when Francis withdrew from the others to pray as he often did, Thomas writes that Francis was "caught up above himself and wholly absorbed in a certain light, the capacity of his mind enlarged so that he saw clearly what was going to come to pass." When Francis returned to the others he told them that, whereas now they were few, "God will make us grow into a great multitude and shall give us manifold enlargement, even unto the ends of the world." In his vision, he told them, he had seen a host of people from every region coming to join them.

Again Francis sent out his brothers, now eight of them, two by two. Francis instructed them to announce to people, "peace, and repentance for remission of sins." He told them that they should teach by example even more than by their words, an issue that he would emphasize time and again throughout his life. He warned them, though, that they would be received by some and rejected by others. Each time he sent people out, he said, "Cast your thought on the Lord and He will nourish you." He said that if asked they should identify themselves as "penitents from Assisi."

As they did the first time, the brothers went about teaching and speaking in cities, towns, villages, and the countryside. Some received them; others mocked. Some thought, by their clothing, that they were wild men, impostors, or fools. People would not invite them into their houses, thinking that they might be thieves, so they were forced to seek shelter in the porticoes of churches and homes.

The situation was made worse by the fact that it was winter and the area was experiencing a severe cold spell. Bernard and Giles, for example, had traveled to Florence. Even though it was bitterly cold, no one opened their doors to them. Finally one woman, who, like the others, didn't allow them into her house, nevertheless gave them permission to sleep on her porch. Many homes kept their bread oven on the porch rather than inside, because of the fire hazard it presented, so the two men could hope to find some residual warmth if they huddled up next to it.

When her husband returned home, however, he angrily scolded her for allowing these people, who were probably thieves or worse, to stay with them. It turned into a typical domestic quarrel, which she eventually won by emphasizing that she had let them sleep outside rather than inside the house, for the very reason he had stated. It just didn't seem right to her to leave any-one out during such cold weather.

The next day that same woman went to church and saw the two brothers there, praying. As she watched, a man who was giving alms to the poor came to the brothers, offering them money. The two men refused, however, saying that they had chosen to live in poverty. In fact, Brother Bernard told him that he had given up much, in terms of personal wealth, to take on this life. The woman overheard this interchange and, deeply impressed, went to Bernard and Giles, offering to let them stay inside her home the next night. The man who had been handing out alms, however, offered them lodging in his house and they accepted his offer. They ended up spending several days with this generous man, talking to him about the Lord.

In spite of this one good experience, however, they were generally treated as if they were "good for nothing." Frequently subjected to mockery and abuse, they were insulted, ridiculed, beaten, bound, or imprisoned. Some were stripped naked and left that way on the public streets. Practicing a variation of "turning the other cheek," they did not ask for their clothing back, although they did take back their clothes if offered. Some of the people who saw how the brothers were reacting to tribulation apologized for the instigators' behavior and the brothers forgave them.[10]

Each instance of abuse and persecution was like a slap in the face after a kind word. They were trying to give something they considered to be very valuable, but their pearls were, as Christ put it, being thrown to the pigs. There was obviously much reason to be discouraged, even to question their calling, but Leo says that the brothers did not become dejected. Instead, they prayed for their persecutors and praised God for providing the temptation that they were able to withstand. They went over the things that they had done, thanking God for what they had done well and shedding tears over what they had neglected to do or done carelessly.

A few days after the brothers returned to Portiuncula, Bishop Guido of Assisi asked to see Francis. Francis had continued to seek counsel from the bishop after his conversion, and the bishop had developed a deep affection for the young man. But he had heard terrible stories about the way Francis and his brothers were being received. He tried to convince Francis to reconsider his refusal to allow ownership and to accept money. Francis responded, "My lord, possessions are often the cause of disputes and sometimes violence. If we owned them we would be obliged to carry arms to defend them—and to do that would hinder us in loving God and our neighbor."[11] Guido, who was, in effect, the wealthiest land owner in the region and who had a reputation for being embroiled in constant litigation to protect his property, found his argument to be disturbingly convincing.[12]

Amazingly, such tribulation did not stop the flow of men wanting to be admitted to their fellowship. They brought some of those they found on their journeys back with them to Saint Mary's in Portiuncula.

The most recent additions to the brothers included Bernard of Viridente, Giovanni di San Costanzo from the villa of that name two miles from Portiuncula, and Barbaro. Little is known about any of these men except that Barbaro became notable for his humility. Then came Angelo di Tancredi, whom we identified earlier as the son of a distinguished consul, a nobleman, a knight who was imprisoned with Francis in the dungeon of Perugia, and who would one day become one of the famous three companions.

In spite of their hardships, the band of brothers was said to remain happy. The three companions report that "nothing could make them sad." They were careful to be generous with the poor, never sending them away empty-handed, even if it meant giving them a piece of their own clothing. "They rejoiced most in poverty," Leo writes, "for the more they were separated from the world, the more they were united to God." They were, in this way, becoming more like the one they followed, Francis, who valued poverty principally because that condition eliminated the "desires of the flesh" from interrupting his communion with God. He was jealous of anything, in fact, that demanded his attention away from God.[13]

Then Francis made a critical move that eventually revolutionized the church. He decided to petition the pope and the curia to grant his group of brothers recognition as an official order of the church. He began to write down a "pattern and rule of life." The stated reason for this decision was that the group was expanding such that it was becoming harder to maintain unity and spiritual stability. The difficulty with this argument is that, at this point in 1209, the group consisted of only twelve men, including Francis. It seems likely that he was also motivated by the persistent mockery and persecution his community of brothers was experiencing. Official sanction by the church would offer a degree of protection against such attacks.

His plan, however, was also dangerous. When Bishop Guido heard that Francis was putting together a set of rules to submit to the pope, he became very concerned and counseled against it. Accepting a life of poverty was not a totally new concept and many movements of that kind had ended up being accused of fostering heresy.

There were many aspects of the church at that time worthy of complaint. Among them was the incredibly lavish lifestyle many of the upper clergy enjoyed, some of whose homes were actually palaces. It was a sensitive task to approach men of great means with notions about the spiritual benefits of a life of poverty.

Francis rarely revealed his thoughts on such matters, but he would have to be very careful in the way he formulated his "rule." The result was a document very hard to refute because it was composed almost entirely of quotations from the Scriptures and heavily based upon the instructions Jesus gave to his apostles. But then that is exactly what Francis wanted to do above all else—to emulate as perfectly as possible the life of Jesus. Almost everything he wrote or said subsequently throughout his life was heavily peppered with Scripture quotations almost one after the other, end to end.

Sometime early in 1209 Francis finished writing his rule, which included the requirements and responsibilities of membership for an order. He then told his brothers that they all needed to go to Rome and tell the supreme pontiff what the Lord was beginning to do through them.

Although Francis would have been the assumed leader in a venture of this importance, before the brothers left for Rome, Francis decided that they needed to choose a leader—a kind of vicar—whom they and he would pledge to obey. They chose Brother Bernard, who had already assumed a position second to Francis. This is the kind of move Francis would make frequently in the future, for the perfect life he had accepted required that he be humble and submissive. In the years that followed he frequently warned his followers to avoid seeking positions of authority. Finally, then, the brothers began the three-day walk to Rome.

THE ROAD TO DESTINY

Rome again beckoned him, but Francis was no pilgrim this time. He was in the eternal city to face one of the most powerful men on earth—a man before whom even the emperor bowed. At his bidding, armies had assembled from every Christian kingdom to rescue the Holy City of Jerusalem from the infidel.

We can question with good reason the exercise of temporal authority by a spiritual body. Christ paid little heed to political issues. His focus was on the inner man and restoring the connection between man and God in every facet of human life. The church was in many ways, however, forced to assume temporal authority during the chaos of the Dark Ages. When secular authority collapsed from the repeated onslaught of invading forces, the only authority left was often that of the bishops and abbots. In their efforts to maintain order and to defend their people, their homes and monasteries were transformed into fortresses and their spiritual counsel into political negotiations.

Instead of St. Peter's, Francis's objective this time was the basilica of Saint John Lateran on the far side of Rome. The

Pantheon, planted around with vineyards, lay a few short blocks to their right as the company of twelve began to walk across the ancient metropolis. Now, more than during his last visit, Francis saw the hundreds of heavily fortified towers emerging like a forest out of the ruins across the forum. A short walk farther on they came to the Palatine, where vineyards snuggled near the crumbling Coliseum, overgrown with vines and weeds. After passing the Coliseum, the brothers bore to their left and saw their destination in a grand complex up against the city wall.

The basilica contained the Papal *cathedra*, which made it the official cathedral of Rome. It was originally built at the beginning of the third century and richly decorated with gifts from Emperor Constantine. These, however, were stripped from it during the series of invasions, and it was almost totally destroyed by an earthquake in 897.

As the group of disreputable-looking men walked up into the loggia, they were surprised to encounter Bishop Guido. The bishop was, at first, concerned at seeing them all there at once, thinking that they were going to leave his diocese. However difficult their reception had been elsewhere, their ministry in and around Assisi had fostered a genuine spiritual revival.

Hearing Francis's intention and probably still concerned about how the pope might react to Francis, the bishop turned to a more influential churchman who was acquainted with the procedural and political complexities of the church: Lord John of Saint Paul, cardinal bishop of Sabina. Francis had heard of him and had gained the impression that the cardinal bishop shared some of his beliefs, "both despising earthly things and loving heavenly things."

They stayed with the cardinal several days; during which time the Lord John tried to gain an understanding of their motives and intentions for this new order. The strict requirements of their vow of poverty concerned him. He suggested that Francis consider taking a less drastic pattern of life, perhaps following the life of a monk or a hermit. Francis would not bend on the matter, however, pointing to the many unique aspects of his proposed order.

The cardinal couldn't help but be impressed with the young man's determination and spiritual fervor, so he offered to be their procurator (their agent) at the curia.[1] He would prove to be a very valuable ally indeed. The cardinal also asked the brothers if, as a favor, they would consider permitting him to become one of the brothers, a request they happily granted.

Lord John did as he promised and brought up the subject of Francis and his plans with the curia. He went so far as to say something very daring: "I believe that the Lord wills, through him, to reform the faith of the holy church throughout the world." Needless to say, the pope was astonished by such an introduction and asked to have Francis brought before him.[2]

Before becoming Pope Innocent III, this small but reportedly handsome man had been John Lothar, count of Segni. He had gained a reputation for keeping tight control of public spending while, on the other hand, giving lavishly to the poor. Francis was probably also impressed with his candor about the state of the church. In an effort to stimulate reform, he had written a scathing, no-holds-barred indictment of the clergy:

"Many priests have lived luxuriously. They have passed the time in drunken revels, neglecting religious rites. When they have been at Mass, they have chatted about commercial affairs." He indicts them, as well, for leaving "churches and tabernacles in an improper state." They have "sold posts and sacraments, promoted ignorant and unworthy people to the clerical state, though they had others better suited for it. Many bishops," he added, "have appropriated the income of a parish for themselves, leaving the parish indigent. They have gone to the enormous abuse of forcing parishioners to make special payments so as to have still more income. They have made a scandalous commerce of relics. They have allowed the illegitimate children of a canon to succeed the father in the benefice."[3]

When it came time for Francis to meet this forceful and direct man, he and his companions were taken to the pope's residence in the Lateran Palace next to the basilica. They were led up an ornate flight of stairs. As they passed through the corridors, they saw two impressive halls. One, called the "Triclinium," had three apses, one at an end, the other two opposite each other in the middle of the room. The walls were very high and decorated with impressive columns. This is where the pope entertained emperors after their coronations. The other was a vast conference chamber, which had eleven apses, a large one at one end of the room and five smaller ones along each side, facing one another. There were also several arcades with extremely heavy pillars.[4]

Finally they were brought into the Hall of Mirrors. It was a dazzling room, which probably featured arched windows facing identical arches enclosing large mirrors on the opposite wall. Francis and his brothers found themselves facing the pope along with an assembly of judges and cardinals. It was an imposing congregation, all wearing their miters and brilliantly colored vestments of white, crimson, and gold.

Francis, of course, was not as fashionably attired. According to witnesses, he looked "despicable" in his "uncouth habit, long beard, unkempt hair and black drooping eyebrows."[5]

Regarding this momentous audience with the pope, Thomas merely says that the pope granted their request and "carried it into complete effect." But others describe the occasion as being far more tumultuous. The pope, they say, flew into a tirade when he saw how disreputable the brothers looked. He commanded Francis to "go and find some pigs, as he was more fitted to consort with them than with men." The pontiff, now standing, gestured angrily toward the world outside. "Roll with them in the slough, give them a rule devised by you for them, and try out the office of your preaching on them!"[6] The grand room was in an uproar as the twelve were roughly rushed out.

It wasn't exactly the reception Francis had hoped for. Bishop Guido and Cardinal Lord John were undoubtedly dismayed. Without argument, however, Francis humbly left.

Bonaventure wrote that the pope was later troubled about the event. Unsure of what he should do, he paced uneasily about in the great mirrored hall. That night God gave the pope a vision. He saw a palm tree sprouting between his feet and growing before him until it was a fine tree. As he pondered this vision, the meaning suddenly became clear: the palm tree was the beggar he had turned away the previous day.

The next morning he gave his servants orders to search for the disheveled and dirty young man. They found him in Saint Anthony's hospice. Once again, humble Francis stood before the lordly assembly of church leaders all regaled in splendor. This time, though, he was not only dirty, he stunk. Francis had done as the pope had commanded and wallowed with the pigs. He stood before them now "covered in filth!" The pope must have stared at him incredulously, hardly believing that this unlearned youth would again appear before him in such an insolent manner.

Francis humbly said, "I have done what you ordered. I beg you now to hear my petition." The pope felt ashamed when he realized that the young man had merely obeyed his orders. He gave Francis his blessing and signaled for him to speak. Francis bowed in gratitude and told him of his plans, imploring him humbly but insistently to approve the rule.

The pope dismissed him to deliberate but then stopped the young man and asked about the harsh nature of the life he was proposing. The pontiff and some of the cardinals had found the rule Francis proposed to be very difficult, perhaps even beyond human strength.[7] The pope conceded that his zeal and that of his companions demonstrated that they were capable, but he was concerned about those who would follow them. Francis remained steadfast, but the pope asked him to pray about it.

Francis again did as the pope requested and received an answer to his prayer in the form of a parable. The next day he told the parable to the pope. Thomas, Leo, and John of Perugia all relay the contents of the parable, but they vary on some of the details. Taking a little bit from all three versions, the story essentially goes as follows:

There was a beautiful woman living in the desert who was dearly loved by the king. The king married the beautiful woman, believing that she would give him many fine sons. She did, indeed, bear him several fine sons, but they all were growing up in the desert without him. She eventually began to worry how she, a poor woman, could take care of so many boys. She, therefore, encouraged some of her sons to go to their father for their inheritance. The king recognized that they resembled him, and he welcomed them into his palace. He then sent word to the woman in the desert to send him all her children, assuring her that they would all be cared for. Francis interpreted this parable as meaning that he was the woman in the desert and that the Lord was telling him that he would take care of all of his sons.[8]

The members of the curia were reportedly impressed by this story, but doubts about the severity of the rule remained a sticking point. John of Saint Paul stood and argued the issue skillfully, "We must be careful. If we refuse this beggar man's request because it is new or too difficult, we may be sinning against Christ's gospel, because he is only asking us to approve a form of gospel life. Anyone who says that a vow to live according to the perfection of the gospel contains something new or unreasonable or too difficult to be observed, is guilty of blasphemy against Christ, the author of the gospel."[9]

The pope then remembered a dream he had had before Francis arrived. In the dream, the church of Saint John Lateran was about to collapse, but a small, shabby-looking man was holding it up. Now he realized that the small man was Francis. He concluded that this holy and religious man, Francis, was the "one through whom the church of God will be sustained and supported."[10]

The pope finally assented to Francis's request. Francis chose to call their order the "Order of Lesser Brethren," which became more commonly known as the "Friars Minor." They were minor "because they were to be subject to all and to do work which made them humble." The pope encouraged the entire group of twelve, saying, "Go with the Lord, brothers, and, as He will see fit to inspire you, preach penance to everyone. When almighty God increases you in number and grace, come back to us. We will grant you more, and entrust you with a greater charge."[11]

There is a hesitation in this statement that could be interpreted as "Let's see what happens." The rule was not formally granted. There was no document that could be displayed, but Francis seemed content to accept the pontiff's word.

Before they left the palace, the pope had the brothers tonsured—that is, the crown of their heads shaved. As a common designation for clerics, this act underscores one of the main reasons that Francis and his brothers attained official sanction while other groups with similar goals did not: Whereas many of these other movements were highly critical of the church and the clergy, much of the criticism probably well deserved, Francis refrained from taking a critical stance against the church. He was quite aware of the corruption. He must have winced seeing the opulent lifestyle of many of the church leaders, among them Bishop Guido and Cardinal Lord John, but he always instructed his followers to be respectful of the clergy, even priests who were known to be venal.[12]

Their walk back to the valley of Spoleto must have been accompanied by a riot of singing and dancing. They couldn't have helped but fear the outcome of Francis's petition. What if their new way of life had been declared heretical? What would they have done then—hide in the hills and go to some place where no one knew them? But they had been approved and joy was the food for the day. They found a place to rest that first night but discovered that they had nothing to eat; however, they were still living on adrenaline and good cheer. In fact, they must have been even further elated when a man they did not know came to them with bread and then went away. For Francis and the brothers, it was a time of miracles.

The next day they continued on until they came to an abandoned place near the city of Orte. They liked the location and remained there about fifteen days, learning more of what it was like to live in poverty. Every once in a while, one of them would go into the city to find provisions. Eventually, however, Francis began to fear that, if they remained longer, it would be interpreted that they owned the place. Non-ownership was an issue that Francis would have to struggle to retain as a rule for the order throughout his life. Thomas states Francis's attitude toward ownership very succinctly: "The followers of most holy Poverty, having nothing, loved nothing and therefore had no fear of losing anything."[13]

In practical terms, however, that meant that they were frequently homeless. Their next stop was Rivo Torto, where Francis, Bernard, and Peter had stayed back in the beginning. As it was one of his father's properties, Francis knew that there was an abandoned shack where they might be able to live. The setting was beautiful with willows and poplars, but the brothers soon began to look upon the shack as a forsaken hovel.

It could, in fact, be more correctly described as a cowshed, often muddy and with walls so tattered that the wind passed through almost unhindered. It was also so small that they could hardly all sit or lie down at the same time. Francis finally resorted to writing their names on the beams above, effectively giving them assigned seats. They often had no bread and lived on a diet of turnips, which was all they were able to get by begging. They slept on beds of straw, sometimes covered with rags or sacks, listening to the sounds of foxes and owls and maybe even the howls of wolves searching for prey.[14]

They were still in that hovel in September when Otto of Brunswick, who would become crowned Holy Roman Emperor Otto IV a month later, passed by along the nearby road. Most of the brothers decided to avoid this display of worldly pomp, but one of them went out and, much like the radicals and eager young Christians of our own day, shouted to the emperor that this glory of his "would endure but for a short time."[15]

The brothers continued to endure the conditions in Rivo Torto until one day a man created considerable disturbance when he forced himself and his donkey into the already overcrowded shack. Looking upon them as property owners, he thought they might be interested in enlarging their abode—a service he would be glad to provide. Francis, of course, wanted nothing to do with owning property or paying for anything or being disturbed in his prayers by "seculars." The brothers returned to Portiuncula.

Francis considered Saint Mary's church in Portiuncula to be more loved by the Virgin Mary than any other place in the world. One of the brothers had a vision in which all the people of the world were blind and surrounding the little church, kneeling and holding hands. With their faces looking upward they were praying for God to give them sight when a bright light came down from heaven.[16] This then is where the order called the friars minor had its beginning—twelve brothers at the church of the virgin mother in Portiuncula.

THE POVERELLO AND
THE FRIARS MINOR

Francis and his ragged group of brothers attracted much attention from the locals when they traipsed along barefoot in their patched-up tunics. It is difficult to understand why anyone would give up all of his possessions—sometimes a virtual fortune—to live in hovels, wear only a ragged tunic, feed on garbage, and be constantly subjected to humiliation and persecution. What did the brothers hope to gain from all these sacrifices? Were they really the fools people thought them to be?

It was certainly not an easy life. Francis allowed each brother to have one tunic with a hood and another without a hood. If necessary, a friar could have breeches with a cord wrapped around his waist. He wanted them all to be clothed "with mean garments," even mended and patched with a combination of sackcloth and other pieces. They were to look abject and vile and therefore "as crucified to the world."[1] No mention is made of how often they bathed or cleaned their little mound of wretched clothing, but it is probably safe to say that cleanliness was not particularly close to godliness in those days.

Francis had grown up surrounded by finery, always choosing the richest garments and the showiest accessories—a man of fashion and extravagant taste. Even his armor and knightly attire were more showy than practical—ostentations in the extreme. But all of that he now saw as vain and worthless, taking his cue from Jesus, who pointed out that "those who wear expensive clothes and indulge in luxury are in palaces" (Luke 7:25). In other words, real people—in particular, the people of God—have better things to do than engage in ostentatious display.

Francis was often referred to as the Poverello, which is the diminutive of "the poor one." Francis was therefore "the little poor one." He referred to poverty as his "holy spouse." He was so devoted to "her" that when he was invited to a lavish dinner with lords, he would first beg some scraps of bread from neighboring houses. When asked why he did this, he would answer that "he would not give up a permanent inheritance for a fief loaned to him for an hour. It is poverty," he said, "that makes us heirs and kings of the kingdom of heaven, not your false riches."[2]

His concern for the *minores* of this world was limitless, as his regular care for lepers dramatically illustrates. He was known to give away pieces of what he was wearing rather than allow someone who asked for alms to go away empty-handed. When a mother of two brothers came to Francis asking for alms, Francis asked Peter of Catania to give her something. He answered that they had nothing except a New Testament. Francis then asked Peter to give the New Testament to the woman so that she could sell it. This was done even though it was the first New Testament in the order.[3]

Francis would not allow the brothers to revile anyone who asked for alms. When one of the brothers accused a man of pretending to be poor, Francis told the friar to strip naked, kiss the poor man's feet, and beg pardon. Francis often said, "Who curses a poor man does an injury to Christ, whose noble image he wears, the image of him who made himself poor for us in this world."

Following the example of Bernard, the first to take on the life Francis espoused, every man admitted to the order was required to sell all of his possessions and give the proceedings to the poor. Some applicants tried to get around this rule. When Francis was preaching in the Marches of Ancona, east of Umbria, for example, a man came wanting to join the order. As usual Francis ordered the man to give away all he had to the poor, but the man secretly gave everything to his family members. Francis learned about his action and, when the man returned and spoke of how generous he had been, Francis laughed and said, "Go on your way, brother fly [his name for money], for you have not yet left your home and your relatives."

On the other hand, Francis learned that he had to be flexible in enforcing this requirement. Once when he was passing a village near Assisi, a young man who was plowing in the field came to him wanting to become a brother. Francis told him that he had to give away everything he owned. The man, whose name was John, gave Francis his ox. What Francis did not realize, however, was that John's parents and small brothers were watching from the window of their humble home. They were very poor and when they saw John hand over the ox they ran out their door in a panic, pleading that they could not survive without the ox. Francis gave the ox back to them in exchange for John, whom Francis would soon call "John, the simple." Although he was indeed "simple," he became a special companion to Francis, known for comically trying to imitate everything Francis did.

Like most common folk, the brothers rose with the sun and went to bed when it set. The daily rules of behavior were very strict—especially in the beginning. No one dared to discuss worldly matters. Francis would not allow secular persons to visit Portiuncula, because he didn't want the brothers to be paying heed with "itching ears" to the things of the world. In fact, the brothers rarely spoke unless they had to and they avoided jesting or speaking idle words in public so that they could not be mistaken for engaging in scandalous or unseemly behavior. Many members of the curia, as well as the local clergy, were still opposed to the friars minor. Some still thought them to be heretical in spite of the pope's endorsement. The friars therefore made every effort to give no cause for complaint and to show themselves in no way opposed to the doctrines of the Catholic Church.

For most of the friars minor, especially those who came from noble and wealthy backgrounds, living in poverty did not come easily. Candles and oil for lamps were luxuries they could rarely afford, so there was no reason for staying up after dark, except, of course, to pray. Little effort was made to obtain comforts. The nights on the plain below Assisi could be quite cold in winter and buzzing with flies and mosquitoes during the summer. When the bishop of Ostia came to visit them at Portiuncula one time, he was moved to tears when he saw that the brothers both ate and slept on the floor. Many of the friars spread hay or rags on the ground beneath their tunic to sleep on, but Francis refused to place anything between his tunic and the ground. He was even known sometimes to sleep sitting up.

Francis always said that "one ascends to Heaven quicker from a hovel than from a palace." Their regular shelter was to be as crude and simple as possible, while on the road they were to seek humble lodging with a priest or in a leper house or tucked into a cave or a porch.[4]

For many of the friars the most difficult aspect to a life of poverty was the necessity of asking for alms. Brothers often felt ashamed to go out and beg for the things they needed. We may remember that even Francis, in the early days after his conversion, was self-conscious about being seen begging. He therefore tried to explain that since "we have chosen the way of poverty out of love for him [Christ]; we should not be ashamed to go out to beg for alms." Although many would question his interpretation of the Scriptures on the matter, he insisted that Jesus lived on alms: "our Lord Jesus Christ, the Son of the Living and Omnipotent God, set his face 'as a hard rock', and was not ashamed, and was poor, and a stranger, and living on alms—he himself and the Blessed Virgin and His disciples."[5]

Francis conducted a kind of training seminar to break through their hesitance to ask for alms. He sent his brothers out individually to surrounding towns, telling them that they "ought to go begging more willingly and with more joyful hearts than someone who is offering a hundred silver pieces in exchange for a single penny." He insisted that "you are offering the love of God to those from whom you seek alms." Taking his cue from the beggar who came into his shop when he was a boy, he told them to say, "Give alms to us for the love of the Lord God!" One argument he used to encourage them was his insistence that by begging they were offering the opportunity for people to do good deeds, "for all that men leave in this world shall perish, but for the charity and alms-deeds they have done they will receive a reward from God."[6]

In subsequent years, some factions of the medieval church would take this concept into questionable corners of doctrine to justify the existence of the poor. Long after Francis's death, Giordana da Pisa included the following quasi-feudal concept in a sermon: "God has ordained that there shall be rich and poor so that the rich may be served by the poor and the poor supported by the rich, and this regimen is common to all peoples. To what end are the poor ordained? To enable the rich to gain eternal life through them."[7]

There was one other caveat to begging as the friars were to practice it: They were not allowed to receive money. Food, supplies, other provisions, and barter items were acceptable but not money. It is difficult to see how Francis derived this rule from Scripture. He may have believed that money most directly symbolized greed and all the carnal affectations that it purchased, or he may have been reacting against his father's total investiture in obtaining money. Francis was very adamant in saying that "money should be no more important to a brother than a stone." The brothers were, however, allowed to receive money when money was necessary to care for the sick, especially other poor people.

Francis's commitment to the life he prescribed for his

brothers is nowhere better illustrated than in his ban on money. He wrote, "Any brother found with money or coin is to be regarded as a false brother, a thief, a robber, and one having a purse, unless he should become truly penitent."[8] One time a secular person came to the church of Saint Mary (Portiuncula) and left money as an offering. One of the brothers touched the money and threw it on the window sill. When Francis heard about it, the brother threw himself on the ground in front of him and was willing to suffer stripes. Francis upbraided him severely and finally told him to take the money in his mouth and to place it on the dung of a donkey outside.

Francis maintained strict discipline in all matters related to the rules. If brothers engaged in idle talk, they were punished. Frequently the punishment involved some creatively penitent action that made the error very graphic, as he had done with the money and donkey dung. Every act was disciplined, writes Thomas, until the senses had been so subdued that they heard or saw little but what their purpose demanded.

This might seem overly severe to most of us, but obedience is crucial to the functioning of any ascetic order. The practice of assigning behavioral rules, usually a form of self-denial, is called *asceticism*, although the practice existed long before the derivation of the word. It could be found in the sands of Ancient Egypt and today in many groups and religions besides Christian. The word actually comes from the Greek *askesis*, which refers primarily to athletic training. The rules were not an end in themselves, but exercises designed to help a person attain more perfectly the virtues of Christian life.[9] For a friar or monk to disobey the rules would be tantamount to an Olympic sprinter refusing to perform the exercises required to develop running skills.

When asked about perfect obedience, Francis likened it to a dead man who can be moved to and fro without complaining and who does not care where he is taken. He further explained, "Take up a dead body and lay it where you will. It does not resist, beg to be moved, complain of its position, or ask to be left alone. If lifted on a chair it does not look up but down; if clothed in purple it appears paler than before."[10]

Strict discipline was also applied to their prayer life. Most people have experienced a time when they had difficulty keeping awake and when falling asleep could prove embarrassing. Prayer was especially important to the friars and their prayer time could last an hour or more. To keep sleep from interrupting their prayers they configured ways that might seem comical to us. Some strung themselves up awkwardly with ropes; others surrounded themselves with iron devices, which would immediately awaken them if they doddered against them. Still others shut themselves in wooden cages, which made sleeping too uncomfortable.

In spite of the strict nature of their rule and the discipline instituted, Francis was reportedly well-liked by the brothers. Thomas describes him as being "generally serene, charming, affable in conversation, faithful in what was entrusted to him, cautious in counsel and even effective in business"—the latter being, no doubt, one of the few gifts contributed by his father. He had a "sweet disposition, a sober spirit, was contemplative and fervent in all things." His discipline was moderated by a predisposition to pardon and an aversion to anger. Thomas also writes that he had a "ready wit," a "tenacious" memory, was "subtle in discussion," and "circumspect" in making decisions. He was kind, cheerful, "immune to cowardice," and "free of insolence." He was able to "fit in" with about any group of people—"more holy among the holy and as one of the sinners when he was with them."[11]

The gentle aspect of his leadership frequently came to the fore at the most unexpected times. Francis knew that the strict daily regimen he imposed upon his followers could become overwhelming. One night a brother suddenly cried out when they were all sleeping, "I am dying, brothers; I am dying of hunger." Immediately Francis got up, prepared food, and commanded that the table be set. He began to eat and told the others to join him, that way avoiding singling out and embarrassing the one who had cried out. He then told the brothers "that to deprive the body indiscreetly of what it needs is a sin."

Francis encouraged each brother to take care of his body so that "it would not murmur and detract from their prayers." With himself, however, he was unrelentingly severe. "He subjected his own innocent body to scourging and want," Thomas wrote reprovingly, "multiplying in wounds without cause."[12]

The friars soon began to regard their spiritual father with a sense of awe. Francis was thought to be able to read their hearts and explore their consciences. It seemed that he often knew what absent brethren were doing and when everything appeared to be going well, he could foretell the approach of evil.

One night Francis was away from the others about midnight, as he often was, praying. Some of the friars were sleeping and others were praying when a fiery chariot of dazzling brightness came through the door of the house and turned about this way and that two or three times. Above it was a huge globe, like the sun, which "lit up the night. The brothers wondered what it meant and finally concluded that it was the soul of their holy father [Francis] which had shone with such dazzling radiance."

All of this adoration, however, never burnished his ego. Humility was the linchpin of a life of poverty. The brothers were now known as the "friars minor." Francis chose the word *minor* (or *minores*) because poverty to him meant not just the absence of things, but a state of mind where a brother accepts a status that identifies him with the lowliest and most despised in society. It was a poverty of spirit, which made them willing to be "subject to all" and to do menial work. In his "rule" he used the words of Jesus to make his point: "whoever wants to become great among you must be your servant, and whoever wants to be first must be your slave" (Matt. 20:26–27).

Francis went to extremes to be an example to the friars in humility. He refused the conventional title of "prior" and adopted "minister" or "servant" instead. He also frequently washed the feet of his brothers and expected them to do the same for each other.

Francis wanted to be regarded as nothing more than one of the brothers. Although he was clearly the leader of the group, to remain humble, he appointed one of the brothers, Peter of Catania, to stay with him as his guardian and master—his vicar, as he referred to him, a person that he would be bound to obey. Not long thereafter he would go further, resigning the office of superior of the order in a chapter meeting and giving it over to Brother Peter of Catania, whom he implored them all, including himself, to obey.

Francis was never comfortable when people praised him or the work of his order. When they did so he might say, "I can still have sons and daughters; do not praise me as being secure. No one should be praised whose end is yet uncertain." When clerics and others would introduce or speak well of him at some gathering, he would whisper or signal to one of his brothers and order the friar to revile him harshly to oppose "the lies" of the men who were praising him.[13]

Among his Admonishments Francis wrote, "Thus may the servant of God know if he has the Spirit of God: if when the Lord works some good through him, his body—since it is ever at variance with all that is good—is not therefore puffed up; but if he rather becomes viler in his own sight and if he esteems himself less than other men."[14]

Brother Leo became Francis's most consistent companion. He accompanied Francis to the Holy Land and was with him at many of the most critical events during his life. He was of noble heritage. Once when Leo was walking beside Francis, who was riding a donkey (which happened more frequently as Francis's health began to fail later in his ministry), Leo became envious. He thought to himself that he was a noble whereas Francis was not, and that their families had never mixed. Somehow Francis sensed what he was thinking, for he got off the donkey and kindly offered the opportunity for Leo to ride, giving him the very noble/commoner reasoning Leo had been thinking. Stricken with guilt, Leo threw himself on the ground and begged forgiveness.

As the order grew, Francis became increasingly troubled when he saw brothers pursuing offices of authority. He had written in his rule that the brothers "are not to exercise power over others" and hoped that his example would stop the practice. He desired people in the order "who would seek not display before men, but glory before God . . . who are not puffed up by such a thing when they have it, but are humbled, and who are not dejected when it is taken away, but are filled with joy."[15]

Ironically, Francis discovered that even poverty had its temptations. There were times, in fact, when Francis seemed to act the part of a jealous spouse to his Lady Poverty. If Francis saw anyone poorer than himself, he was immediately "envious, and, in the struggle to achieve complete poverty, feared to be outdone by another."[16] But then he would recognize the pride in his thoughts and become mindful that there were people who were poor not by choice and whose lives depended upon alms. Francis claimed that he always took less than he needed so that the poor would not be cheated of their share. "To act otherwise would be theft," he said.

Whether this statement comforted the poor is questionable, but again we need to realize that, while Francis had deep compassion for the poor, the poverty he chose was not a decision primarily designed to bring attention to the plight of the poor or to improve their condition. The friars did that, of course, by ministering to the poor in sickness and in need, but they did not strive to lift them out of poverty. Poverty was a way of life for the brothers that was designed to deliver them from slavery to the things of this world and to bring them closer to God.

More controversial was his view that education was detrimental to a fittingly humble life. Francis said that a great cleric must, in some way, give up his learning when he came to the order. In the first place Francis regarded learning as a possession that an applicant needed to renounce like any possession. Second, he thought that "learning takes from many people their docility . . . and does not permit them to bend to humble practices." Francis believed that the day would come "when knowledge would be an occasion of ruin, but the striving after spiritual things would be a bulwark of safety to the spirit."

That last contention does not seem to have been borne out over the centuries, but he was right in looking upon education as a possession in which people took pride and often used to elevate themselves above those with less or no education. But education was gaining ground as an important attribute for members of the clergy. More and more bishops, cardinals, and other clerics were studying at the University in Bologna and other places. Many of his staunchest supporters among the clergy opposed him on this issue. Their influence proved to be so great that education eventually became a hallmark of the Franciscan community.

Some would say that Francis took the concept of humility too far. According to Thomas he, in fact, strove "to attain perfect self-contempt," and he instructed his followers to likewise "despise themselves." But, as we noted earlier, Francis was not fostering insecurity, self-doubt, or depression. Thomas gave us a clue to his true intentions when he wrote that "more and more did Francis come to despise himself" until finally, with the help of God, he "attained to perfect conquest of himself."[17] Francis looked upon his body and his inner self almost as separate entities, the former demanding things—fine foods, luxuries, pleasures, etc. It was *that self* he wished to conquer—its demands he wished to subdue. The clamoring of all these

things distracted and barred him from what he loved most—
being with his Lord.

He had been a slave to that self during his youth—indulg-
ing in every vice that a person demanded. He was to spend
much of his life using measures of fasting, denial, and bodily
mortification—measures we would consider extreme and
which probably played a part in bringing about his premature
death—to conquer it.

Admission into the order of friars minor required a vow of
chastity. "The Rule and life of these brothers is this," Francis
writes to introduce his rule, "namely, to live in obedience and
chastity, and without property, and to follow the doctrine and
footsteps of our Lord Jesus Christ."

Francis commanded his brothers to avoid familiarity with
women. "A woman was so unwelcome to him," writes Thomas,
"that you would think that his caution was not a warning or an
example but rather a dread or a horror." Thomas goes on to say
that Francis had difficulty speaking with them and would not look
at them. When he talked to a woman, he also spoke loudly so that
no one could misinterpret his intentions. Thomas adds his own
opinion that "there is no profit in looking at women." He considered doing so to be, at the very least, a waste of time, and provides
"an impediment to those who would walk the difficult way."

To illustrate Francis's aversion to women, Thomas tells of
two spiritual women in Bevagna, who, at the request of Francis's
companions, brought food to them. He repaid them with "the
word of God" but would not look at them. According to Thomas,
Francis often said that "all talk with women is frivolous except
only for confession."

This portrait of Francis having an extreme aversion to women is questionable. This is not to say that Francis had no apprehensions about women. This was the Middle Ages, after all, and he was allied with a church governed by professed celibates. He had no choice but to be concerned about how the public perceived the order in the light of the intense scrutiny they were under. In addition, since Francis had spent the first half of his life being anything but chaste, it was a powerful element of that "self" that separated him from God and that he wanted to discard. It was his adversary or at least a weapon of his adversary, which he as the knight of Christ had to defeat.

All of the brothers had the onerous task of fighting off temptations of the flesh. Abstinence from food was one method, but efforts could involve stripping themselves naked out in the cold or piercing their bodies with thorns, sometimes drawing blood. Francis was so earnest to avoid fleshly temptation that in winter he would plunge into a pit full of ice until he was free of the temptation.

On one occasion, while he was at the hermitage of the brothers of Sartiano, Francis felt himself being tempted with lust. When he realized it, he took off his clothing and beat himself very severely with his cord, saying, "See, Brother Ass, thus is it becoming for you to remain, thus is it becoming for you to bear the whip." "Brother Ass" was the name he applied to his carnal and rebellious body.

When the temptation did not go away, in spite of the scourging that had left his body marked with welts, he went out into the garden and cast himself naked into the snow. He set up seven snowballs and referred to them as sons and daughters and wife and servants of the evil spirit. He then commanded the spirit to clothe them, for they were dying from the cold. The devil is said to have "departed in confusion."

Francis came to believe that the safest remedy against the snares of the enemy is "spiritual joy." "The devils cannot harm the servant of Christ when they see he is filled with holy joy." Whenever he felt dejection coming over him, he would pray for the restoration of "the joy of salvation."

The truth, though, is that Francis enjoyed a very close, comfortable, and chaste relationship with a young woman named Giacoma de Settesoli. She was one of the richest women in Italy. A resident of Rome, her husband, Graziano, was a member of the very powerful Frangipani family who opposed the papacy. Her husband, however, died in 1212 or 1213, leaving her with two young sons. Soon thereafter she heard Francis speak and was converted. She adopted Francis and his friars as one of her charities, setting up a house for them in Rome and later a church. Francis called her Brother Giacoma, and although he would have taken measures to avoid any implication of impropriety, he visited her on many occasions, enjoying the treats she often made for him.

There was also another woman, one highly revered on her own merits, whose name is rarely spoken without reference to Francis. She was called Clare.

CLARE: LADY OF LIGHT

Tradition called for ladies to be elegantly dressed as they took their seats in churches and cathedrals on Palm Sunday. In a sense Palm Sunday was a rehearsal for the highest of holy days that would come one week later: Easter. Palm Sunday, though, was a more relaxed holiday. As if by decree, people were to be happy. Clouds were not supposed to gather overhead except for maybe a few feathery light patches here and there, their shadows chasing each other across the mountain amid the wildflowers. The Palm Sunday of March 18, 1212, in Assisi was not going to follow tradition, however, for a pretty, blonde teenage girl named Clare.

According to the story she was sitting on a bench in the Cathedral of San Rufino. High above her head, pointed arches, an innovation in a time when semi-circular Romanesque arches were still the standard, paraded behind her toward the incomplete facade. Under construction now for more than seventy years, the church would require as many more years before it was completed.

Sitting with Clare were her sisters, Catherine (later called Agnes) and Beatrice, as well as her mother. At one point during the service worshippers were supposed to rise from their seats and go to the altar, where they would receive a palm branch. Her mother and sisters complied, but Clare remained in her seat crying. Seeing her distress, Bishop Guido took a palm branch, circled around the altar, and went to where she was seated, offering it to her. She took it, but continued to cry.

That night, after dark, Clare, shaking with fear and anticipation, put on her walking shoes and her cloak, quietly left her room, and nervously crept down the steps of her family's fortified tower palazzo. Finally reaching the lowest level, she tiptoed down the corridor to a small, concealed door. People called it the death door since it was through that door that the dead were removed from the house. Fearing that any moment she might wake up one of her uncles or cousins, she fumbled to loosen the iron bolt on the hidden door and slipped out of the house.

The moonlight shadow of the cathedral next door loomed over her as she hurried down the lane. A short distance away, she was joined by two or three close friends who had promised to help her complete a daring mission. One was probably a woman named Pacifica; the other may have been her cousin Rufino, who was now one of the friars minor. They crossed through the piazza in front of the cathedral, circled around the building for the canons, and passed through the San Rufino gate. Illuminated only by fleeting patches of silvery moonlight, they made their way through the woods and down the hill along a network of lanes until they reached the road that would lead them to Portiuncula.

Francis and a number of the brothers were waiting for her.

Given the solemnity of this momentous happening, they might have met her in the woods, carrying torches, and processed back with her to the little chapel. Francis snipped off long strands of her beautiful golden hair, performing a rite that was a bit unorthodox, given his position, but one that symbolically wed her to Lady Poverty.

Knowing that she couldn't possibly stay with the brothers at Portiuncula, Francis led her and her friend on a two-mile walk past the dry River Tesio, which ran north of Assisi toward Gubio, to a little Benedictine monastery on the banks of the Chiagio named San Paolo delle Ancelle di Dio. More commonly known as "San Paolo delle Abbadesse" (Saint Paul of the Abbesses), it was known for its wealth and "noble status."

~

Clare was born in 1193 or 1194, which made her about eleven or twelve years younger than Francis. The Bernadones lived in *il sotto*, while Clare's family, the noble Favorones of the house of Offreduccio, lived in *la sopra* near the piazza of San Rufino, the exclusive section of town claimed by the nobility.

Clare's grandfather, Offreduccio di Bernardino, was a powerful count who had at least three sons: Scipione, Monaldo, and Favorone di Offreduccio, the last being Clare's father. All of them were knights—a family descended from the Lombards and Franks who invaded Umbria centuries before. Their valor, ruthlessness, and fighting skill were well respected and feared. Clare's father was known for riding into battle with his sword drawn. As feudal knights, they were supportive of the emperor against the claims of the papacy. Clare's mother, Ortolana, was also of noble lineage, linked, in fact, to the line from which the future emperor, Frederick II, was descended.[1]

Clare grew up in an atmosphere of violence. The entire feudal system was under attack by the communes. In response, the emperor and his feudal lords ruthlessly ravaged cities, murdering, torturing, and raping their citizens to stifle the rising opposition. She was a small child when Assisi burst into civil war in 1198, and she stared out her tower window in terror at the smoke-filled city. She could hardly understand what was happening during those nights red with fire as one after another of the great houses was burned and battered to the ground. She may have seen Francis among the merchant rebels, running through the streets, throwing torches into houses and yelling anti-*maiores* slogans. The Offreduccio family with five-year-old Clare left for Perugia just before their house next to the cathedral was razed.

While Clare was exiled in Perugia, her mother educated her in Latin, history, and the poems of chivalry. Clare was reportedly quiet and demure, spending most of her time at home. Like Francis, she often set aside food for the poor.

Exactly when Clare and her family were able to return to Assisi is unclear. Some maintain that it wasn't until 1207, after Francis's conversion, while he was busy repairing and rebuilding the churches. Others believe that she returned in the early stages of his conversion.

A pair of sculpted stone lions guarded the doors to the new cathedral, San Rufino. During his conversion, Francis is said to have stood on top of the lions to preach to people in the cathedral's piazza. Clare could have witnessed this scene from a window. In either case, sometime, either from his preaching or his wild words in the streets, Francis caught her attention.

Some information about Clare comes from the investigation that preceded her canonization. Lord Ranieri di Bernardo said that she was strikingly beautiful and was being groomed for marriage in her early teens. He and others say that she was one of the most sought-after noble maidens. Although she was solicited by many suitors of high rank—Ranieri among them—she rebuffed them all.[2]

In the meantime, her family and the nobility in general were feeling their grip on power again slipping away. In spite of their victory at the battle between Perugia and Assisi and the "Peace Paper," which had forced the commune to restore their homes, the nobles and feudalism suffered another blow in 1210, when a treaty was signed in Assisi that stipulated that the *maiores* give up their domination of the *minores* who, under the feudal system, had been personally dependent upon them. The citizens of Assisi were, therefore, no longer "someone's men"—no longer subject to forced labor imposed by the nobility upon the serfs. The men of the commune and the obligation of one man to another disappeared in favor of a dependence of the individual on the community. Ironically, the true *minores*—those living outside the city in the rural areas—were not included in the treaty.[3]

As anger in the Offreduccio family toward the *minores* was again rising, one of their own shining offspring was considering abandoning her class altogether. In 1211 Clare became anxious to meet with Francis, but that was unthinkable for a high-born girl of her age, or at least it was supposed to be. She began to sneak off and have secret meetings with Francis and Philip the Long.

A witness at Clare's canonization proceedings said that Francis's complicity in Clare's conversion was public knowledge. Witness #17 in the canonization proceedings was Lady Bona, daughter of Guelfuccio of Assisi. She testified that she accompanied Clare on clandestine meetings with Francis, "so as not to be seen by her parents." The same woman also testified that Clare gave her money as a votive offering and directed her "to carry it to those who were working on Saint Mary of the Portiuncula so that they would sustain the flesh."

Clare's sister Beatrice, who would later join her, testified at her sister's canonization that her sister left the family at the urging of Francis. "He went to her many times," she said, "so that the virgin Clare acquiesced, renounced the world and all earthly things and went to serve God as soon as she was able."[4]

Some maintain that Clare's relationship to Francis was much deeper than is indicated by the scenario above. In fact, some witnesses say that Clare and Francis were meeting clandestinely during the early years of Francis's conversion between 1204 and 1205. Some scholars maintain that Francis's "best friend" was actually Clare.

At the same time, Francis's friends were increasingly preoccupied with the question of whether Francis was going to take a wife. Even before that, in his famous vision of a grand palace filled with implements of war, Francis saw, seemingly out of context, a "beautiful bride."

Did Francis have a real woman in mind during this time? Had his friends noticed him meeting secretly with a woman and therefore come to believe that he was involved with her romantically? Could she have been this "best friend" and his first follower, her identity hidden because of her youth and gender? Those reasons could also explain why she could not immediately join him and why, even later, Thomas and his three friends might have disguised her identify for fear of bringing scandal upon her memory.

When Francis, while repairing the church of San Damiano, cried out that this church would become a monastery for ladies, did he have Clare in mind? In her own testimony, Clare says, with what could be interpreted in a sense of loving amusement, that she saw Francis shouting about the convent when stumbling about on the roof of the church.

If Clare was indeed his best friend and his first follower, the story would gain another level of drama and romance. But to be considered that friend, several obstacles needed to be overcome. First of all, for her to consistently meet secretly with Francis, she would have had to use considerable ingenuity. Girls in wealthy noble families were guarded very carefully lest they lose their virginity before a suitable marriage match was arranged. Daughters were valuable and often could provide a business or political advantage.

It would have been scandalous for Francis and Clare to be seen together anytime alone. Meetings at church or in the market when Clare was with her mother, a nurse, or some other authorized adult would have been acceptable. There may have been more formal social engagements where they could contact each other—at parties, weddings, and festivals.

Most significant to the issue is the age difference. Lady Bona said that "at the time [Clare] entered Religion, she was a prudent young girl of eighteen years." When asked how she knew that,

Lady Bona said that she "used to converse with her."[5] This corresponds with the most reliable research, which places Clare's birth on July 16, 1194. But given this birthdate, Clare would have been only ten or eleven years old at the time Francis was meeting with his "best friend" at the cave.

Francis was between twenty-two and twenty-four during his conversion. At ten years old, Clare could have hardly been a romantic interest. She might, however, have been a tagalong, a little girl who had been taken by the young knight in shining armor—the popular young rake people were always talking about. Of course, even that kind of relationship might have planted the first seeds of conversion.

Needless to say, Clare's proud and powerful family did not let this breach of familial ties go uncontested. A few days after her arrival at San Paolo, on the morning of Good Friday, Clare heard a disturbance outside the monastery. A group of her relatives had arrived and were knocking at the door. They were admitted and allowed to meet Clare in the church, where they were dismayed to see her dressed in the shabby habit of a friar. They pleaded with her to return, but she refused and the argument became heated. When the family determined to force Clare to return home, she ran to the altar, holding on to it for refuge. Although threatened with sacrilege if they touched her while she clung to the altar, they circled around her like wolves until she pulled off her head covering to reveal her shorn hair. They hesitated and then the nuns came in and shamed them into leaving.

The knights returned again for another tussle with their kinswoman and were again forced to leave empty-handed. The nuns at San Paolo were becoming increasingly troubled, however, by the repeated conflict with such a powerful noble family and, given the informality of Clare's vow, urged her to seek shelter elsewhere. Francis then took her to the monastery of Sant'Angelo di Panso, located on the slopes of Mount Subasio. It was not as beautiful a setting as San Paolo. It was dry and seemed forbidding beneath an overhanging cliff.

Two weeks after Clare's daring break from the family, her sister Catherine (Agnes), in a similar act of stealth, joined her at the convent. "The Legend of Saint Clare" records, "The next day, hearing Agnes had gone off to Clare, twelve men, burning with anger and hiding outwardly their evil intent," ran to the convent and, feigning a friendly demeanor, managed to convince the ladies to let them enter. Having given up on reclaiming Clare, they concentrated on Agnes, asking her, "Why have you come to this place? Get ready to return immediately." When she refused, one of the knights began to hit and kick her. He tried to drag her away by her hair, while the others pushed her and lifted her into their arms. They rushed out of the convent with her kicking and screaming. Clare begged them to release her, but they continued to carry Agnes along the slope of the mountain, the bushes and trees and rocks tearing at her clothes and hair as she struggled. People working in a nearby field heard the shouting and cursing and ran up to the banner of knights. They dropped Catherine, now unconscious, on the ground, and her uncle Monaldo, having sworn to bring her back dead or alive, drew his sword and prepared to kill her. To the amazement of the onlookers, so the story goes, his arm froze when he held his sword high and he was not able to move it until they left her and walked away.

Neither Clare nor Francis had any intention of leaving

Clare in a pre-existing convent. Clare was a follower of Francis, and her chosen way of life was to mirror his life. She couldn't, however, live among the brothers; she had to have a place of her own and for her sisters and other women who might decide to join them. Francis had already prophesied that San Damiano would be that place.

It had usually been assumed by scholars that Clare had to wait several years before San Damiano was converted into a suitable place for a convent. However, Father Marino Bigaroni, in his research as an archival and architectural scholar, proved that work began almost immediately after Clare's conversion. The crypt of the little church was filled in and a cloister was built on beside the church, providing a kitchen and a refectory. Clare quickly decided it would be unsafe for the sisters to follow the example of the friars and go out begging for food. Two friars—"questors" they were called—were assigned by Francis to live in shacks outside the walls of the church and to do the begging on their behalf.

Thomas refers to Clare as "noble by family, but nobler by Grace; a virgin in her flesh, most chaste in her mind; youthful in age, but hoary in spirit; steadfast in purpose and most ardent in longing after the Divine; endued with wisdom and eminent in humility, bright (Clare) in name; bright in life; brightest in character."[6]

It wouldn't be long before Clare's second sister, Beatrice, would join her and even her mother, Ortolana, eventually became one of the "Poor Clares." In fact, one by one, in the succeeding years, daughters of the nobility all over Assisi abandoned their families to join her. One named Cristiana, the daughter of Cristiano, a consul of Assisi, joined Clare at San Damiano, where she felt "consoled by Clare's daily conversations with her." In the canonization procedures for Clare, Christiana testified that she "believed that everything that could be said about the holiness of any holy woman, even of the Virgin Mary, could be said about her."[7]

When he was in Assisi, Francis visited Clare often and consoled her. Sources say that she needed consoling and that only Francis could provide it. Francis was very protective of her, however, and would not let her go beyond the cloister, which may indeed have been one reason why she needed consoling.

Sometime early in her life at San Damiano, Clare requested the opportunity to share a meal with Francis. She, in fact, asked him several times to give her that consolation. But Francis always refused. As usual, Francis was concerned about his example to the brothers. They were expected to avoid unnecessary interaction with women. How could he break his own rule and expect his brothers to abide by it faithfully? It was his brothers, however, who finally convinced him to grant her request.

Realizing how much Clare would appreciate the opportunity to be relieved of her confinement even for a short time, Francis arranged for her and a select few of her sisters to come to Portiuncula and share a meal. The dinner was carried out in an almost chivalric manner, with Lady Clare seated first—on the ground, of course—and then Francis and then another lady followed by another friar in decorous procession. There were no banners waving, no crystal or silver catching the candlelight, no servants parading in with fine gourmet delicacies from France, and both the knight and his lady were dressed in rags. But for one brief, shining moment, Francis was the knight and Clare his lady.

A VOICE IN THE WILDERNESS

In every society we look for our heroes to be the most beautiful or handsome, the strongest, the tallest, the wisest, and the bravest. Except for the last two, Francis was none of these. He is never described as being handsome or good-looking, although all his preening and ostentatious dress may have made him more appealing to women as a youth. Thomas describes Francis in amazing, almost clinical, detail. He is thought to have met Francis face-to-face when he was admitted to the order by Francis himself at San Maria de Portiuncula sometime between 1213 and 1216.

Thomas writes that Francis was of average height or maybe a little under, which means that he was short. His head, too, was of average size and round, although he says Francis's face was "a bit long and prominent" beneath his black hair. Francis had a smooth and low forehead with eyebrows perfectly horizontal above his black eyes. Between those eyes his nose was "symmetrical, thin and straight." His teeth were "close together and white" behind small, thin lips. He had a black beard but it was not "bushy," Thomas says. His temples were smooth and his ears were set "upright but small. . . . His neck was slender, his shoulders straight, his arms short, his hands slender, his fingers long, his nails extended." His legs were thin, his feet small, and his skin "delicate."[1]

Of course, the fame Francis would eventually gain was not based upon his physical attraction. After one of Francis's successful sermons, a friar named Masseo, born a nobleman, brought up that very question. "Why does everyone want to see you, hear you, follow you, obey you? You're not much to look at, you are not aristocratic and you're not even very well educated." Francis kneeled down and answered, "I think it must be because God has chosen me, as the most worthless and inadequate sinner on earth, to confound all presumptions of nobility, pride, power, beauty and worldliness."[2]

Francis was a preacher—a very good one. He was generally friendly and cheerful and had a nice, clear, peaceable voice— "strong, sweet, and sonorous," as Thomas describes it. He was eloquent, in spite of his minimal education, and often witty, although he could become fiery and sharp when he denounced to their faces men known to be guilty of greed, exploitation, and cruelty.

His descriptions and illustrations of evil, courage, and other Christian and non-Christian attributes were colorful, since he could work in all his memorized scenes from the Arthurian romances and the *Chansons de Geste* as well as draw from the behavior of the animals he was growing to love. As a poet, words and images came easily to him. He instructed his friars to use similes rather than abstractions. Some people said that he could also "make a tongue of his body," using theatrical gestures and imaginative props to grip the attention of his audience.

Francis rarely spoke from behind a pulpit, especially in the early years of the order. In the countryside Francis would preach to laborers, their families, and landowners while standing atop a bale of straw or in the doorway of a granary atop a barrel. In town piazzas he would climb up on a box, a cart, or the steps of public buildings. Drifters assembled as did clerks and women from their houses, even priests, sometimes even the seigneurs and magistrates, to hear him speak.

The secret of his success, Thomas writes perceptively, was that Francis "looked upon the greatest multitude of people as one person and he preached to one as he would to a multitude." He did not plan what to say when he preached. Sometimes, when nothing came to him, he would just bless the people and let them go, believing that the blessing would be good enough.

Francis said, "The preacher must first draw from secret prayers what he will later pour out in holy sermons; he must first grow hot within before he speaks words that are in themselves cold."[3]

"He spoke filled with the Holy Spirit," Thomas writes. His enthusiasm for the message he presented was boundless. One time when he went to Rome on some business regarding the order, Francis wanted to speak to the pope and the gathering of cardinals. When Francis came before this exalted assemblage, he humbly asked for permission to speak and, after receiving it, began to preach. He was so animated and fervent in the outpouring of words that "his feet moved as if he were dancing."[4]

Clerics and laypeople alike began to desire entrance into the new order. Among the newest crop of brothers was Rufino di Scipione. He was Angelo's oldest friend and Clare's cousin, coming from the very powerful Offreduccio family. Like Clare he was taken by his uncle, Monaldo di Offreduccio, to Perugia during the civil war. He was young and often tongue-tied but may have influenced Clare into taking the bold move of leaving her family to adopt the life of poverty Francis espoused.

Leo came along with Rufino. He was a priest from Assisi who would become Francis's confessor and constant companion. Twenty years after Francis died, Leo, Rufino, and Angelo collected their memories of Francis, which Leo transcribed onto the scrolls referred to many times previously in this work—sometimes known as the *Scripta Leonis* or *The Legend of the Three Companions*.

Francis was not always so fortunate in his choice of novitiates. One brother seemed to be perfect in every way, seeking silence and rejoicing in the Scriptures. The other brothers admired him greatly and some even referred to him as a saint. Francis, however, sensed that something was amiss, that the brother had a worldly desire to be special, to be admired, an attitude that Francis was well qualified to detect. He told the others that his judgment on this matter was based upon the fact that the brother never confessed. He suggested that his skeptical brothers ask the man to confess and see what happened. His admiring friends did so, halfway kidding, and, sure enough, he refused to confess. He kept on avoiding confessing and later left the order.

Thomas writes that "above everything else, Francis thought that the faith of the holy Roman Church was by all means to be preserved, honored, and imitated, that faith in which alone is found the salvation of all who are to be saved. He revered priests and he had a great affection for every ecclesiastical order."

It is difficult to know how Francis actually felt about the church since all of the early biographies were written at the behest of the clergy. Yet it is true that Francis became deeply loved and admired by many bishops and cardinals, including Bishop Guido of Assisi, Cardinal Lord John of Saint Paul, and two men who would each become Pope—Honorius III and Gregory IX. In a statement that rings true to Francis's personality, he said, "We have been sent to help the clergy toward the salvation of souls so that what might be found insufficient in them might be supplied by us." If they are not as good as they should be, it is up to God to deal with them. "Hide their lapses, supply for their many defects; and when you have done this, be even more humble."[5]

As we noted earlier, the priesthood was immersed in a sea of corruption charges, many of which are verifiable through a review of court records in cities all over Italy. Francis was willing to overlook the sins of priests, however, because of the miracle of their office. Although the doctrine of transubstantiation was not widely accepted at the time, Francis was constantly awed that a priest literally "administered the most holy Body and Blood of our Lord Jesus Christ." Consequently he believed that "the sin of those who offended against them [priests] is greater than any against all the other men in this world."[6]

On the other hand, Francis was also regularly distressed by the way priests treated what he saw as the body and blood of Christ. He criticized their carelessness several times in his writings: "They wrap it in dirty linens" or "poorly maintained challises," which are "carried away disrespectfully and administered indifferently. Shall we not by all these things be moved with a sense of duty when the good Lord Himself places Himself in our hands and we handle Him and receive Him daily? Are we unmindful that we must needs fall into His hands?"

It became standard practice that whenever the brothers saw a church they were to bow down toward it flat on the ground and worship God, saying "We worship Thee, O Christ, [here] and at all Thy churches." Likewise, whenever they encountered a priest, rich or poor, they were to bow to him and bless him.

Although Francis was devoted, at the cost of his own health, to caring for the poor and to encouraging all others to do the same, his "Lady Poverty" was not a political statement. She defined a way of thinking and acting to which he was committed, body and soul.

Poverty served a very practical but important function in Francis's spiritual life. He did not want to need things. To need something meant that he was "subject to it," "yielding obedience to pleasure." To free himself from a desire for good-tasting food, Francis rarely ate cooked food, and if he did, he would often mix it with ashes or quench its flavor with cold water. When he ate with secular people who gave him delicious food, he would only eat a little, saying that he was fasting. If invited to dine with a great prince, he would do so and would even eat meat, since he knew that Jesus did so, but after fulfilling the minimum, he would only pretend to eat the rest, letting it fall discreetly into his lap.

Things also made demands that separated Francis from his Lord. He tried to shut off everything in the world that would distract him from his attention to God. Truth be told, it was not only his desire for humility that drove him to choose others to lead the order, but his desire for solitude. The demands of organization and shepherding stole from him time he would rather devote to communing with Christ.

Francis made a project of discovering secluded places for prayer—hermitages as they became called. Everywhere he went about Umbria and Tuscany preaching to the people, he looked for more hermitages. As people began to hear about his desire for these secluded spots, he began receiving gifts of land to use for hermitages. At each one a group of three of four brothers would set up housekeeping as a base for ministering to the surrounding areas.

The Benedictines offered Francis their hermitage on Subasio, close to the caves of his early conversion—known as *I Carceri* or The Cells. From Assisi you can reach the spot by traveling along a path in the woods that eventually joins a road and then a track winding up through the forest from the abbey of San Benedetto. Adrian House said that in the dim light "a blue and white haze of anemones spreads over the forest floor" accompanied by the melody of a stream splashing down into a gully.

When Francis was in a village named Greccio in the beautiful Rieti valley, the story goes that he was so fond of the village that he asked a young boy to throw a stick (or a chunk of coal), promising to build a hermitage wherever it landed. The stick struck a sheer cliff wall on the side of a mountain. Giovanni di Velita, Lord of Greccio, immediately turned over the mountain to Francis to be made into a hermitage. Francis eventually had four hermitages in the Rieti Valley.

Pretty soon hermitages were everywhere that Francis went. There was Celle near Cortona, the Carceri on Mount

Subasio, and the more solitary hermitages like Los Speco. One of his hermitages near the top of Monteluco in a dark ilex forest was visited by Michelangelo in the sixteenth century at the age of eighty-one. Some have said he was a member of an offshoot Franciscan order, called the third order.

Francis didn't pray for just a moment, nor did he pray idly, but he prayed intensely for long periods of time. If he began late, he might not finish praying much before daylight. Francis had a habit of spending the whole day in his cell, coming out only when he needed something to eat, and these were not regular times. His brothers were used to eating without Francis when he did not respond to their signal that a meal was prepared. Even when he was at the table eating, he could be caught up in some meditation about the Lord and stop eating. At such times no one was allowed to disturb him.

When Francis was praying at Portiuncula one time, Bishop Guido of Assisi came to him for a friendly visit and walked without being called into where he was praying. He stuck his head in and saw Francis praying and was suddenly overcome and began to tremble. His limbs became rigid and he could not speak. Then he had a sense of being driven out by force, pushed back some distance. He returned to the brothers, began to confess the wrong he had done, and recovered his speech.

Sometimes when Francis was traveling and felt the Spirit, he would drop behind the others and stand still to receive the inspiration.[7] If the Lord came upon him in public where there was no private cell, he made a cell of his mantle. If he did not have a mantle, he would cover his face with his sleeve. "Always he put something between himself and the bystanders, lest they should become aware of the bridegroom's touch." If there was no other option, he "would make a temple of his breast," presumably bowing his head and praying quietly.

Francis would return from his private prayer and try to fit in with the people so that no one would notice his inner fire and ruin what he had received through their overt reaction, often expressed through unwanted compliments. Francis said that when someone comes away from prayer, "he should show himself to others as poor and as a sinner, as though he had attained no new grace."[8]

For Francis, prayer was the core of his life—not prayer as a stiff recitation of thanks and requisitions, but the joining of himself with Christ. Such devotion is difficult to communicate and difficult to understand. To what can we compare it that does not, in that comparison, demean it? Some, for example, might say that prayer was like a narcotic to him, giving him an incredible "high." But for Francis the high was not an end in itself. He looked for opportunities to pray as if it were a romantic encounter.

When Francis prayed in the woods and in solitary places away from the noisy traffic of mankind, "he would fill the woods with sighs, water the place with his tears, strike his breast with his hand and often speak to his Lord out loud." Thomas says that he became "himself a prayer."[9]

Even in his praying something of the dashing troubadour was always present in Francis. His thoughts and his words held echoes of music in his mind. Sometimes when he was overcome by "a sweet melody of the spirit," he would speak about it in French, even sing it in French. Other times he would pick up a stick and pretend it was the bow of a fiddle. Then he would pantomime playing it as he sang in French about the wonders of his Lord.[10]

GROWING PAINS

amine. The winds of want blew hot and dry across the land when Francis was born. For more than five years the fields were barren of produce, and what grain could be scratched out of the hard soil was nearly worthless. Hunger stumbled through the parched streets and groveled in the water-less ditches. Driven by unbearable hunger, people resorted to eating the tawny wild grasses and died. Records in the Assisi archives describe this period as *il tempo della fame capitale*, "the time of the capital [deadly] famine."[1]

In the medieval mind everything that happened in the spiritual world was reflected in the physical (or vice versa). Hence one could expect these catastrophic conditions to indicate turmoil and devastation in the spirit of man. Writing about this time, Thomas adopted a biblical turn of phrase. "The people of Assisi had forgotten the ways of God and had neglected his commandments."

But then something happened. Francis happened.

"Thus it came to pass," wrote Thomas, "that in a short time the face of the whole province was changed, and she appeared of more cheerful countenance, the former foulness having everywhere been laid aside. The former dryness was done away and in the field erstwhile hard the crops sprang up quickly; the untended vine began moreover to put forth shoots of divine fragrance and, after bearing blossoms of sweetness, yielded fruits of honor and virtue together."[2]

Friars walking barefoot along the roads in northern Italy became a familiar sight. They worked with their hands, comforted the sick, and helped the needy, their pay a crust of bread or a bowl of soup or a covered space to rest their heads. Their message was simple: do penance and turn to the Lord. In spite of the harsh life, the order grew and their missions forged across Italy, beyond the Alps to the north and the sea to the south.

Francis, still much a white knight in his mind, began looking across that sea toward the lands of the Saracens. It was a place where heroes fought and died to wrest Jerusalem from the hands of the infidel. He too could fight, though as another kind of knight, offering life instead of death. A few months after Clare's conversion, in September of 1212, Francis and a brother—perhaps Leo or Peter—set out eastward, across Umbria and the Marches of Ancona to the region's port of the same name: Ancona. There they boarded a ship bound for Syria. Winter had already begun to stir the waters of the Adriatic and a violent storm arose. Their ship was whipped and driven off course, until it plowed into the rocks along the shore of Dalmatia. They survived, only about ninety-five miles from where they had boarded ship, but on the far side of a sizable body of water.

Francis found another ship bound back to Ancona and

begged a group of sailors to take them along. But the men insisted upon payment—money, which the brothers did not have.

"Trusting in the Lord," wrote Thomas, they risked stowing away on the boat. Before the ship embarked, however, an unknown man came aboard and gave a crew member provisions to pass on to Francis. The crewman did so without letting the other sailors know of their presence. The ship left port, but another, even more violent, storm arose. The sailors fought the wind and waves for days. Then their food supply ran out. It seemed as if they were at the mercy of the turbulent waves until Francis revealed himself and offered to share the provisions provided by the mysterious stranger. Though slight, the rations proved sufficient to sustain the crew and their passengers until they reached port. Once in Ancona, the sailors thanked God for saving them through his servant, Francis.

Before they began the fifty-eight mile trek back to Portiuncula, Francis spent time in Ancona, speaking to the crowds of people milling along the docks and in the streets. Many were disenchanted; those lost and fleeing their old lives—"fleeing the world," as Thomas put it. Many of them, rather than seeking a new life in foreign lands, chose to follow in the life of Francis.

Francis had no intention of giving up his ambitions toward the Holy Land. Every bit as fearless as he had been battling Perugia with a sword, he was now anxious to rain blows upon the infidel with the Scriptures. A year or so after his first attempt, another opportunity arose.

The latest crusaders had succeeded in driving the Saracens out of southern Spain. Francis and Bernard wanted to use that opportunity to travel to Barcelona, where they hoped to get a ship bound for North Africa. Their objective to visit was the nazir Miramolinno who had now set up base in Morocco.

It was a long way to Barcelona by foot. They would have to take the Via Francesca up through Pisa and then travel the long, winding line of the coast from Genoa through Marseilles and Narbonne. He could have abbreviated the trip by taking a ship out of Genoa directly to Cadiz, from which they could easily reach Morocco. But then Francis's aborted voyage to and from Ancona may have dampened his interest in sea travel.

Francis didn't seem to mind the extra time. Others joined the two friars on their way, making a merry company of travelers. Thomas wrote that Francis was so anxious to reach their destination that he walked far ahead of his companions, "drunk" in spirit with the anticipation of encountering the Saracens. On the brink of fulfilling his hopes, Francis became ill. His health had remained fragile ever since his ordeal in the dungeon. Some witnesses say that he lost his voice, but the only thing that mattered to Francis was that God was calling him back. His mission to the Saracens would have to wait.

Francis and Bernard decided not to immediately return to Assisi. Instead, they forged into Spain. The record is unclear; perhaps they joined a pilgrimage to Santiago de Compostela. When they finally decided to head homeward later in 1213, they crossed the Pyrenees along one of the pilgrimage routes and picked up the road that Francis had traveled with his father. Pietro, however, was now on his deathbed. His name disappears from all records in Assisi and is replaced by that of his younger son, Francis's brother, Angelo.[3]

Back home, increasing numbers of women, inspired by the

work of Clare, were joining her "poor ladies," which was also referred to as the second order of the friars minor. A significant segment of the population, however, was excluded from membership in either of the two orders. These were the married couples. Although unable to break their marriage vows, they were drawn by Francis's message and wanted to live according to the life that Francis described. To answer this need a third order was established, according to which couples vowed to practice penance in their own homes under the guidance of designated brothers. They were more formally called the "order of penitents."[4]

The original order continued to draw converts, of course. Not long after Francis returned from Spain, Thomas of Celano, his someday biographer, appeared at Portiuncula and was accepted into the order by the hand of Francis himself. He was a priest, scholar, and highly regarded professional writer.

Another convert was Brother Elias, an Umbrian school teacher. Actually his full name was Elias of Bonbarone, a family name that appears among the nobility in Assisi's early documents. A legal document dated December 9, 1198, describes Elias of Bonbarone as a "forceful and self-confident" man who once served as first consul of Assisi.[5] He is thought to have studied law at Bologna and would ultimately become head of the order after Francis's death.

Brother Pacifico, born in Ancona, was a colorful convert. He had been a composer of erotic songs and the best known troubadour in Italy, the equivalent of a rock star in our own time, one whom Francis may have admired in his youth. Pacifico had, in fact, been crowned King of Verses by Emperor Otto.

In spite of these developments, the order was still

experiencing growing pains. There remained considerable opposition to the order among leaders of the church. Thomas wrote, "O how many, above all, when these things were first taking place, were plotting to destroy the new Order that had been planted! O how many were trying to choke off this new choice vineyard."[6]

A significant crossroads was reached when Pope Innocent III sent out a call for the Fourth Lateran Council. The princes of the church converged on Rome from all over the Christian world, their colorful trains snarling street traffic, filling every available place of lodging, and attracting crowds of peddlers and beggars and sellers of refreshments and souvenirs. Innocent III convened the Fourth Council in the Lateran basilica on November 11, 1215. Francis was among those present although without having the minimum required status of a prior, he was not allowed to cast a vote.

Among the seventy items on the council's agenda was an announcement that no new orders would receive formal authorization. This measure was purportedly enacted to contain the flood of dissidents and the appearance of movements potentially hostile to the church's teaching authority. There was also a declaration that, in the future, aspirants could only enter a religious order that was established with a secure and regular income.

These measures appeared to sound the death knell for the friars minor. Francis had nothing in writing to authorize his order. Even if the pope's unofficial blessing was accepted, that would not cover the poor sisters at San Damiano, and, of course, both groups were penniless.

Francis appealed to the word of the pontiff as justification for the official status of his new order, and Bishop Guido worked feverishly behind the scenes to ensure the acceptance of his plea. He succeeded in eliciting from the pope a declaration in council that Francis's order had been officially authorized. The problem of the "poor sisters" was set aside for another day.

During the time of the council, Bishop Guido introduced Francis to Cencio Savelli, who would succeed Innocent III as pope. He had given away most of his wealth while auditing that of the entire church. He was sympathetic to Francis's commitment to apostolic poverty and assured Francis of his support.

Bishop Guido also introduced Francis to Ugolino dell Conti di Segni, Innocent's nephew who would also one day be pope and prove to be a significant supporter of the order. Ugolino was known to be a clever theologian and an expert lawyer but had a fiery temper. However, he was genuinely moved by Francis's transparent goodness.

Ugolino, for his part, introduced Francis to Dominic, the other noted traveling preacher of the day and future saint. The bishop wanted to deter Dominic's desire to establish another order by convincing them to join forces. Ugolino's thinking was that they could both adopt a modified Augustinian rule, which Dominic already professed. The two future saints had a zeal for the Lord in common, but their lifestyles were very different. Francis would have to soften his stand on poverty, a compromise he was not willing to make.

One of the other declarations that came out of the council required orders to hold regular chapter meetings. Francis had already adopted this practice. The brothers had assembled twice a year, at Pentecost in May and at the feast of Saint Michael in

September. The friars came from wherever they were, more each year and from farther away.

In the early days these meetings were very intimate and familial. When a chapter ended, Francis would bless the brothers and assign each of them to work in individual provinces. He would also decide who could be preachers. Not all of the friars, he had discovered, were able to prick the hearts of listeners with their words and expressions. But there were many other ways to touch hearts and fulfill needed ministries. The first official chapter meeting, following the directive from the Lateran council, was held on Pentecost of 1216. At that meeting, the order ambitiously planned a number of missions. Francis intended to take part in a mission to France. He selected a group of friars to accompany him and they set out on their journey.

Francis decided to go by way of Florence where the Bishop of Ostia (Ugolino) was staying at the time. He hoped to renew the friendship that had begun to bud during the recent Lateran council. While there he, as a mere formality, asked the bishop's permission to travel to France. He was truly astonished when he didn't get it. The bishop could see no reason for making dangerous journeys to outlying areas. Francis persuaded him to realize that the order was bound to save both clergy and lay people wherever they could find them, but the bishop still thought it unwise for the founder of the order to put himself in harm's way. Francis reluctantly sent the rest of his group on to France without him and remained with the bishop to develop what would become a deep and lasting friendship.

Innocent III, still in his fifties, unexpectedly died on July 16, 1216. Efforts to handle the funeral and the succession were frantic. Fortunately, most of the cardinals were in Perugia where Innocent had been trying to settle a dispute between Genoa and Pisa. The issue concerned the supply of shipping for the crusade he was sponsoring, referred to as the fourth crusade.

It was a hot day and the cardinals and their entourages raced to send word of Innocent's death to all Christendom. In the meantime, his body was robed in his richest vestments; his tiara was placed on his head and his crosier (shepherd's staff) by his side. To the chanting of prayers, he was carried into Perugia's cavernous cathedral where he lay in state among the treasures of his pontifical office.

Early in the morning, however, when the canons opened the cathedral, they found that thieves had broken in and that everything of value had been taken, including the clothes off the deceased pope's back. The pope's body was lying in the middle of the church almost naked and already gathering the stink of death. Francis was said to have taken off his own habit to cover the man's corpse—a tender moment filled with cascading memories of the pope who had authorized his order.

Two days after the death of Innocent III, nineteen cardinals assembled at Perugia on July 18, 1216, to elect a new pope. Due to the conflicts within Italy, the threat posed by the Tartars, and the fear of schism, the cardinals had a sense of being under siege. They therefore agreed, in the interest of expediting the process, to give cardinals Ugolino of Ostia and Guido of Praeneste the power to appoint the new pope. Their choice fell upon Cencio Savelli, the cardinal Bishop Guido had introduced to Francis during the Lateran council earlier. Taking the name of Honorius III, he was consecrated at Perugia on July 24.

By this time, the initial distrust with which many church-men had greeted the work of Francis was beginning to melt. Even some of the most cynical were beginning to believe that the brothers, by being linked with the church, were a positive model for the laity, especially in contrast to the widespread corruption that had previously stymied reverence for the church. Many priests, in fact, had joined the order and others had been reformed by their message. The order was also being increasingly seen as a peaceful channel for many of the controversies that had previously rocked the church.

In 1217 the increasing number of priests in the order allowed Francis to adopt the office, by which the hierarchy of the church set great importance. It entailed saying seven hours or services spread through each day: matins, prime, terce, sext, none, vespers, and compline. Brothers were supposed to attend each of them in the chapel, or, if traveling, to read them "with moving eyes and lips."

The hours were not a mere repetition of phrases. The psalms, readings, and prayers rotated from day to day and with the devotional seasons. They would complete all 150 psalms by the end of each week and the entire Bible every twelve months. Francis also composed his own prayers, psalms, and antiphons for each of the seven services in a cycle he called the office of the passion. Most of them were dictated to Leo.

During that year, Francis agreed at their general chapter that his brotherhood should be divided into twelve geographic provinces, each under the supervision of an elected minister. Although he realized the necessity for the organizational enhancements, Francis was disappointed that he could no longer personally accept each new applicant into the order. Increasingly he heard himself referred to as Minister General or Father rather than Brother.

At the same chapter, the mission to Outremer, referred to in the order as Syria, was assigned to Elias, the former schoolmaster and consul. After the Pentecost chapter in May, he and some companions took a ship for Acre.

In the meantime the other two orders were experiencing expansion. The third order, or "brothers and sisters of penance," was growing rapidly with increasing numbers of married couples vowing to observe penance in their own homes.

Clare, too, was gaining prestige, and her "ladies of poverty" was growing precipitously. Many young women and widows secluded themselves in cities and towns in monasteries established for doing penance.

Eventually Clare was asked to take over houses in Spello and Spoleto. Cardinal Ugolino wrote to Honorius for instructions, because he had been approached with offers for land on which to build houses for holy women in Siena, in Lucca, and at Monticelli near Florence. Honorius gave his consent for all of the projects. Although they started out as places outside the order for women committed to poverty, they soon became associated with Clare, who sent her sister Agnes to be abbess at Monticelli.

In October 1216, Jacques de Vitry, newly consecrated as Bishop of Acre, wrote a letter that described the papal court and the friars in contrasting terms. "I saw much that entirely dissatisfied me; all were so taken up with their temporal affairs, political and legal, that it was almost impossible to discuss anything spiritual." But then he noticed "a great many men and women who have renounced all their possessions for the love of Christ—'Friars Minor' and 'Sisters Minor,' as they were called. They are held in great esteem by the Lord Pope and the cardinals."

"During the day," de Vitry wrote, the brothers "go into the cities and villages, giving themselves to the active life of the apostolate; at night, they return to their hermitage or withdraw into solitude to live the contemplative life. The women live near the cities in various hospices and refuges; they live a community life from the work of their hands, but accept no income." They lived and worked in such a spirit of humility that "the veneration that the clergy and laity show them is a burden to them."[7]

They were soon spreading out across the continent. Thomas of Eccleston in his *Chronicle* described their arrival in England in 1224. In Canterbury, he wrote, they found lodging in a small room under a building that housed a school of priests. At night, when the students went home, the brothers entered the deserted school, where they would light a fire and sit around it.

In Salisbury "they drank round the fire at the time of conversation with such good humor and joy that he was thought happy who could take the cup from his neighbor in jest in order to drink. Like children and young people who laugh every time they meet . . . the brothers, above all the younger ones, burst out laughing at their first encounter."[8] It is a great mystery why people, even those possessing great wealth, would give up everything to live in poverty. Yet the friars minor displayed an uncommon propensity for happiness and multiplied. They had nothing, yet what they had became valued more than the palaces of princes.

14

LEGEND

"Francesco is coming! Francesco is coming!" The news was passed down from one to another until people began rushing out of their homes, shops, churches, and workshops—vendors, peddlers, and magistrates. Even more than the acrobats and troubadours, these days people looked forward to the coming of the Poverello. The people in Ascoli were said to have trampled upon each other in their eagerness to see and listen to him. Thirty men in that city, we are told, "received the Lord that day." Everywhere this little man in rags went, crowds followed. He was no longer just a man. Events in his life began to reach legendary proportions.

Sometime around the year 1212 Francis had come to the town of Alviano, a couple days' walk south of Assisi, to preach. While he was standing on a high place surrounded by the walls of a fortress and overlooked by its turreted towers, his efforts to speak were being hampered by a group of swallows chattering and screeching. Francis finally turned to the birds and said, "My sisters, swallows, it is now time for me to speak, for you have already spoken enough. Listen to the word of the Lord and be silent and quiet until the word of the Lord is finished."

To everyone's astonishment, the birds obeyed, remaining there quietly until Francis was finished. Those who witnessed this said, "Truly this man is a saint and a friend of the Most High."[1]

Of all his attributes, it is his love for the simple creatures of the earth for which Francis is most remembered. Sometime after his encounter with the swallows of Alviano, he and several brothers were walking along a road near Bevagna, not far south of Assisi, where many birds—daws, crows, and doves—were flittering about in the trees. Because, as Thomas says, Francis felt great "tenderness toward lower and irrational creatures," he ran to the birds and greeted them. Surprisingly the birds did not fly away, so Francis asked them to listen to the word of God.

He spoke to them for several minutes, saying, among other things, "My brothers, birds, you should praise your Creator very much and always love him; he gave you feathers to clothe you, wings so that you can fly, and whatever else was necessary for you." He added, "God made you noble among his creatures, and he gave you a home in the purity of the air; though you neither sow nor reap, he nevertheless protects and governs you without any solicitude on your part." Then he made the sign of the cross and walked among them, touching some here and there, until he finally gave them permission to fly off.[2] Since the birds listened to his words with such reverence, Francis, from that day on, spoke to all birds and animals.

Francis later expressed a desire that the emperor make it a law that, at Christmas time, everyone who could would drop corn and grain along the roads so that the birds would have much to eat, "especially our sisters the larks."[3] People began to envision him with a bird on his shoulder or flying off the tip of his finger and with clusters of rabbits, squirrels, lambs, and other animals cavorting happily around him. It is an image replete with innocence reminiscent of the way such fairy tale characters as Snow White, Cinderella, and Aurora (Sleeping Beauty) are portrayed in Disney's classic animated features.

Francis believed that animals had a modicum of sentience. He said that he could "see their obedience." Thomas tells us that Francis "enjoyed such sweetness" when contemplating the wisdom of their Creator displayed in his creatures. He was very often filled with "a wonderful and ineffable joy" while he looked upon them.[4]

Among the stories told of Francis and his fellowship with the animal kingdom is that of a little rabbit caught in a trap near the town of Greccio. The rabbit was set down and came to him when he called it. It remained close to him, apparently recognizing him as a source of kindness and safety. Later when Francis tried to let it go, it kept returning until he finally asked his brothers to take it out into the woods.

On another occasion he was in a boat among the thick reeds and white water lilies near the shore of Lake Lungo, near Rieti, when a man caught a large fish and offered it to Francis. The man must have been bewildered when Francis called the fish his "brother" and placed it in the water. There the fish played happily near the boat for some time until Francis gave it permission to swim away. Francis was particularly drawn to animals mentioned or encountered by Jesus. It is not surprising then that he had a special love for doves and for small lambs since Jesus was so often spoken of as a lamb.

He was said to love even the most humble of creatures. If he saw a worm on the road he would pick it up and move it to safety. While he was in a cell at Portiuncula, a tree cricket in a fig tree caught his attention. He found its singing to be very "tender and sweet." Every day for eight days Francis would come out and command it to sing and it delighted him with its singing. It departed only when Francis gave it leave to go.

Francis, however, was no pantheist. Nature was not God nor did it share in a universal divinity. He viewed the entire panoply of creation as the collective offspring of God. Their beauty was an expression of God's beauty, love, and wonder. His adoration, therefore, was not limited to the animal kingdom. He was moved by the loveliness and fragrance of flowers and spoke to them as if they were endowed with a special intelligence beyond the perception of mortal men. He loved gardens because the sweetness of the smell brought to mind the "Eternal Sweetness."

With all things being in this way the children of God, there was every reason, he believed, to regard them as his brothers and sisters. When he came to a field full of flowers, he would preach to them, inviting them to praise the Lord. He spoke in a similar manner to cornfields, vineyards, and forests—exhorting them all to love God and to serve him willingly.

Francis eventually extended this concept even further to include things that had not even a spark of life—stones, fountains of water, earth and fire, air and wind. He walked reverently upon stones because Jesus was referred to as "the Rock." The brothers were not allowed to cut down a whole tree because

Francis wanted the tree to be able to sprout again. He eventually gave up the use of lights, lamps, and candles because he did not want to extinguish them later. They were a symbol, as he said, of the "holy light which shines eternally."

He went so far as to feel a special affection for anything that reflected in some way the hand and presence of God. He would pick up reverently anything written, whether or not the word of the Lord was on it, because he said that the name of the Lord was made up of such letters and that they were therefore due veneration.

If some of these stories seem to transport him into the realm of fantasy, the many miracles attributed to him suggest a miracle worker on the level of Jesus himself. Ours is a more skeptical age where miracles are concerned. These intrusions into the natural order of things are eagerly sought by some and regarded with suspicion or even scorn by others. This is not to say that Francis performed no miracles at all, nor can we presume to make judgments regarding the veracity of this or that miracle, but it is interesting that in none of his writings does he mention performing miracles. He may, of course, have omitted mentioning them due to his humility, but it may also indicate that his proclivity for miracles was less than his legend suggests. All evidence points to the fact that he did not like to draw attention to himself or to his level of spirituality. A degree of objectivity should be maintained.

Miracles were often attributed to the things Francis touched. When he blessed bread that someone brought to him, people who afterward ate it were reportedly cured. The same was held to be true if somebody touched any object he touched or drank water into which his cord belt was dipped. Some people told of being cured when they just touched his tunic, so it is not surprising that people often tore off pieces of his tunic. After his death miracles were reported as happening at his tomb, when he appeared to people in dreams, and when people merely spoke his name.

One story tells of a pregnant woman who went into labor and stayed in it painfully for days. Having heard that Francis was coming their way, the people of the village hoped that he would heal her, but he ended up going another way. He had, however, taken ill and had borrowed a horse to ease his travel. After his safe arrival at Portiuncula, he assigned a friar to take the horse back to its owner. The friar happened to take a route through that village and was taken aback when people suddenly rushed toward him. They were disappointed, at first, when they discovered that the friar was not Francis, but when they learned that Francis had ridden the horse, their hopes revived. Selecting something that Francis might have touched, they removed the bit and reins from the horse and ran to the pregnant woman. When she touched them, so the story goes, she gave birth happily.

Many of the reported miracles mirrored ones that Jesus performed. When Francis was in Narni, for example, one of the brothers had what Thomas calls a "falling sickness." This may be likened to a situation Jesus faced when confronted with a man possessed by a devil. Following the model of Jesus, Francis delivered the troubled man—one of his followers, we are told— of his tormenting spirit.

One can detect echoes of the miracle of the loaves and fishes when Francis once visited the city of Siena. The pope and many cardinals also happened to be there, many of whom came to visit Francis while he was staying in the house by the modest church of San Fabiano. Unfortunately, the traffic of clergy trampling through and picking grapes all but ruined a small vineyard next to the house, gravely upsetting the resident priest. It was a small vineyard, but it provided enough wine for his needs. In deep sadness, he told his friends, "I lost my vintage for this year!"

When Francis heard of it, he called the priest to him and told him that the Lord could restore his loss, which the priest told him was thirteen measures. Later, when the priest harvested the grapes, he found that he had twenty measures from what was left. The priest was overjoyed and thanked Francis profusely.

Some of the reported miracles have an epic quality—concerning the welfare of dozens or hundreds or thousands of people, more like the miracles we read of in the Old Testament.

Francis had a vision about evil happenings in Perugia. He went there with his brothers to preach, but knights doing training exercises kept interrupting them. Francis prophesied that because they did not recognize God or give thanks to him for their prosperity there would be civil war. In 1222 the prophecy was fulfilled when the townspeople began fighting the nobles.

Once, when Francis came to Arezzo, just a few miles north of Perugia, he found that city also embroiled in civil war. From outside the city Francis saw devils rejoicing over the city, reveling in the turmoil and destruction they were causing. He called Brother Sylvester and told him to go to the gate of the city and command the devils to leave. Sylvester did as he was asked and "soon thereafter" peace was restored.

One of the most colorful miracles is recounted in *The Little Flowers of Saint Francis*. The story relates how Francis tamed a ravenous wolf that had become a plague on Gubbio, killing both livestock and the people who crossed its path. Francis went out looking for the wolf. It saw him and ran toward him drooling hungrily, but Francis made the sign of the cross and the wolf put its head down and lay before him like a lamb. He condemned the wolf for "destroying God's creatures without mercy" and for killing "human beings made in the image of God." He said that the wolf deserved death for its crimes but that he wanted, instead, to make peace. The wolf's body language suggested that it was willing to consider the idea, so Francis made a pact with the wolf in which it agreed to eat no more animals or humans in return for a daily allotment of food provided by the people.

At Toscanella, a small town several miles south of Assisi, Francis performed a miracle that has a special ring of truth. A soldier there begged Francis to heal his lame son. Francis refused to comply with this request, because he considered himself far too useless and unworthy of such power. His reaction here is more consistent with the humble, self-deprecating man he was. Several times he was asked to heal the boy and each time he declined until he finally gave in and prayed, laying his hand on the boy and giving the sign of the cross above him. The boy, we are told, was raised up and healed.[5]

Francis was much more than the sum of his miracles, however long that list might be. The ability to perceive truths, to penetrate to the core of the human spirit, to find value where none is apparent, and to discern the fake amid the genuine are the hidden gems in his life.

In December 1221 the weather was cold and foggy and it was raining, according to a story told in *The Little Flowers*. Walking along the road from Perugia toward Assisi and Portiuncula,

Francis may have been preoccupied with memories of the Battle of Collestrada years ago fought just off the road and thought how profoundly his life had changed. His breath a white plume in the air, Francis called to Leo, who was walking ahead of him, and asked him to write down what he was about to say. After his eyesight began to fail, Francis relied increasingly on Brother Leo to take dictation when he wanted to write something.

Francis said, "Brother Leo, although the Friars Minor in these parts give a great example of sanctity and good education, write it down and note it well that this is *not* perfect joy." Although puzzled by this sudden outburst, Leo dutifully did as he was told, carefully shielding a scroll of paper in the folds of his cloak.

They walked on a little farther and Francis, once again, called to Leo, saying, "Brother Leo, even though the Friars Minor should give sight to the blind, and loose the limbs of the paralyzed, and though they should cast out devils, and give hearing to the deaf, speech to the dumb and the power of walking to the lame, and although—which is a greater thing than these—they should raise to life those who have been dead four days, write that in all this there is not perfect joy." Again Leo recorded the words of his mentor.

Francis continued to recount similar amazing capabilities for the friars, the final being, "Brother Leo, even though the Friars Minor should preach so well that they should convert all the infidels to the faith of Christ," and, as he had called after all the preceding, Francis called aloud, "write that herein is not perfect joy."

Finally Leo turned to him and said, "Father, I pray you, for God's sake, tell me wherein is perfect joy."

Francis answered, "When we have returned from Perugia to St. Mary of the Angels at night, soaked and frozen and encrusted with mud, and, after I have knocked and called for a long time, a friar comes and asks through the door: 'Who are you?' I answer, 'Brother Francis.' And he says, 'No, you are two good-for-nothings! Go away. You can't come in.'

"And if he would not open the door to us, but left us without, exposed till night to the snow and the wind and the torrents of rain, in cold and hunger; then, if we should bear so much abuse and cruelty and such a dismissal patiently, without disturbance and without murmuring at him, and should think humbly and charitably that this porter knew us truly, and that God would have him speak against us, O Brother Leo, write that this would be perfect joy.

"And if we should continue to knock, and he should come out in a rage, and should drive us away as importunate villains, with rudeness and with buffetings, saying, 'Depart from this house, vile thieves; go to the poorhouse, for you shall neither eat nor be lodged here;' if we should sustain this with patience, and with joy, and with love, O Brother Leo, write that this would be perfect joy.

"And if those inside should finally come outside and throw us down and roll us in the snow and then beat us with knotted sticks, and if we should bear all these things patiently and with joy, thinking on the pains of the blessed Christ, O Brother Leo write that this—*is* perfect joy."[6]

THE KNIGHT OF CHRIST

I t was a time of glorious deeds and infamous betrayals, when greed and ambition raised banners of faith and trampled the faith in bloodied sands. *The crusades*. Infamy has been the heritage of those centuries of warfare, but to the contemporaries of Francis, it was the banner headline of each day's news—a holy war upon which the fate of the world rested. And no man longed more to cross swords with the infidel than Francis.

The first crusade was launched in 1095 to protect the beloved Christian shrines in the Holy Land from the encroachment of the Saracens. It was moderately successful and Jerusalem was secured in Christian hands. Further Muslim expansion, however, provoked the second crusade (1145 to 1148), which tried and failed to regain what had been lost to the Muslims.

Then, in 1187, came the resounding blow. Jerusalem had fallen! That holiest of cities was now in the hands of Saladin, the greatest of the Muslim warriors. Bells tolled across all of Christendom, and every church echoed with mourning and cries for deliverance. When Francis was five years old, the third crusade (1187 to 1191) was born.

Saladin followed up this victory by launching a jihad against all Christians. This challenge brought Emperor Frederick I, or Barbarossa, himself into the field of battle, where he met his death. Jerusalem was not retaken by the Christians in the third crusade, but King Richard I of England, known also as Richard the Lionheart, captured the coastal town of Jaffa and secured some Christian access to Jerusalem.[1]

Shortly after his election in 1198, while sixteen-year-old Francis was dismantling the stone walls of La Rocca during Assisi's revolt against the noble houses, Innocent III initiated the fourth crusade. It was not the best of times. England and France were at war and Germany was embroiled in a power struggle between two claimants to the imperial throne. At the same time a schism had begun developing between the Eastern and Western church (Orthodox and Catholic). The pope's priority called for establishing treaties between warring entities, reuniting the Eastern and Western churches under his papacy, and then, forming a united front, recapturing the holy sites in Jerusalem. He focused his attention on Egypt because it was the primary Muslim power center at the time. But the crusade was waylaid by internal squabbles, disagreements, and power struggles, particularly fomented by Venice, upon which passage to the Holy Land depended. The fiasco ended with a disastrous attack on Constantinople. The army never reached the Holy Land.[2] Needless to say, such sectarian madness did nothing to heal the breach between the Eastern and Western churches.

In 1215 Pope Innocent III began drumming up support for the fifth crusade in an effort to regain what had been lost in the fourth, but he died before the venture was in full force.

It was during the course of this fifth crusade that Francis revived his desire to go to the Holy Land. He was at first concerned that Bishop Ugolino would again forbid him from going. A mission to the Holy Land would be far more dangerous than the one he had previously proposed to France. To his surprise, though, Ugolino encouraged him to go, advising him to take Peter of Catania with him. Francis left the friars in the hands of two relative newcomers: Matthew of Narni was to take charge of the Portiuncula and admissions to the order. Gregory of Naples was to keep an eye on the provinces. The latter, though, would prove to be ambitious, worldly, clever, and sometimes cruel. Rumors suggested that he was another of Ugolino's nephews.

Ten years after the creation of the order, Francis set out for Syria for the third time. Thomas provided few details of this momentous event, so we will have to rely on other sources to fill in the story. Francis sailed for Acre in midsummer, 1219. Many friars wanted to go with him, but the captain limited the number to twelve. Besides Peter of Catania, these included Barbaro, Sabbatino, Leo, and Illuminato, a man who had entered the order around 1210 when Francis and the brothers were still staying at Rivo Torto.

Francis disembarked from his ship at the port of Acre on the coast of Syria. The city lay at the northern tip of a long sickle-shaped bay, its harbor sheltered by a hook of land above which rose massive stone walls, battlements, castles, and churches. The city was spoken of as being quite beautiful, with its many gardens and terraces, Moorish archways, and elaborate fountains. Amid this native beauty were a large number of fortified tower houses like those that dominated Italian cities.

The quays were constantly busy with the arrival and departure of troopships and merchantmen flying banners bearing the colors and crests of an international fleet. There would have been ships from France, Germany, Brittany, Spain, Frisia (a small province near Germany), and Holland, all answering the pope's call to liberate the Holy Land.

Among the soldiers and knights were those whose raised colors represented Italian republics, including Venice, Genoa, Pisa, Lucca, and Bologna. The colors of the Spoleto valley might have been there as well—colors beneath which Francis had once longed to bear arms. On the field of battle in the crusade itself, all of these members of the many nations would bear the same emblem and the same colors on their silks and shields—the cross and shield in crimson on white. Even monks and priests wore that emblem on their habits and mantles.[3]

Francis soon found Elias with his fellow missionaries whom he had sent out to Syria two years earlier. Whether or not Francis knew it, Brother Elias had enjoyed a rich life in Acre. He had lived in elegance and drunk fine wines at a bountiful table. He had gained social status as a respected scholar and philosopher who understood the Muslims. In fact there were reports that, due to his command of rhetoric, eloquence, and persuasive skills, he had converted several Muslims. Eventually Elias would gain a reputation as one of Europe's great intellectuals. He was described as "armed with so much wisdom and so much prudence that he was first among the men of his time, first among the Roman Curia, and much esteemed by the Curia of the Empire."[4]

Anxious to get to the battlefront, Francis went back to the port but was unable to find an available ship except for one whose captain would only take two of them. Francis chose Illuminato to accompany him and asked the others to follow as soon as they could.

The sultan at that time was Saladin's brother, Malik al Kamil, who was in the Egyptian delta near the city of Damietta, protecting his power base in Cairo.

Not far from Cairo the Nile divides, its arteries fanning out, reaching toward the sea in a broad sweep. Francis would have seen them emptying into the Mediterranean all along the coast amid a landscape of low dunes shaded by thousands of date palms as his ship approached Africa. Damietta guarded one of the two main tributaries in the east while Alexandria lay farther to the west.

Francis was welcomed to the crusader headquarters by Bishop de Vitry, who, we recall, had been so impressed with the friars when he was consecrated as Bishop of Acre by the pope three years earlier. Damietta was not a pleasant place in the heat of summer. The inhabitants were afflicted with plagues of flies and epidemics of disease and dysentery. Gangrene rotted the flesh of scores among the wounded, and an outbreak of scurvy had already killed ten thousand.

They could look forward to torrential rains in November as well as a cutting north wind that would drive the water up in piles of waves onto the shore, flooding camps and supplies, leaving dead fish and the corpses of donkeys and horses as well as humans.

King John de Brienne, the brother of Francis's boyhood hero, Gautier de Brienne, was the military commander. In 1210 he had become titular king of Jerusalem when he married

Marie of Montferrat, queen of the crusader state of Jerusalem. He was described as "large, heavy, tall in stature, robust and strong." Some considered him to be so skilled in the art of war as to evoke comparison with the legendary Charlemagne. He would ride through a field of battle, striking with his bludgeon one side and then the other with such power that the Saracens fled as if he were the devil himself. In his time the tides of legend held that there was no man on earth braver than he.

John de Brienne had sometime earlier defeated the Saracens in what was called the Victory of the Tower. Both sides had believed that the key to Damietta was a small island in the adjacent tributary of the Nile. It was linked to the town by a line of boats and heavy chains to block the passage of enemy ships. A tall fortified tower rose from the island, manned by four hundred soldiers and crossbowmen. It was that which King John had finally taken before Francis arrived. As a result of this damaging defeat, the sultan, Malik al Kamil, was ready to concede Jerusalem to the Christians. The conquest seemed to have been won.

Unfortunately, Cardinal Pelagius, the arrogant personal representative of the pope, who all too often preempted the plans of the king, had greater ambitions. Cardinal Pelagius was described by one historian as a "fanatical Spaniard, fiercely impressed with his own rank." He refused the sultan's terms and demanded that the Muslim leader surrender all of Egypt along with Jerusalem. Not surprisingly, the sultan refused. Consequently, when Francis arrived at the camp, the cardinal's forces, having rebuffed the sultan's offer, were poised to attack Damietta. The city was well fortified, however, with walls and towers and protected by a river and a moat.

King John had set up what appeared to be a very effective blockade and favored patience to allow their blockade to work. Cavalry charges, he knew, were completely useless here amid the dunes and marshland. But the rank and file soldiers, overwhelmed by pestilence and plague and anxious to get home, were on the brink of mutiny, accusing their superiors of cowardice. Pelagius took the side of the men and, overstretching his authority, ordered King John to attack.

Francis, more trusting of the king than the clergyman, became very concerned about the safety of the men and prayed all night. In the morning he told Illuminato, "The Lord showed me that if the battle takes place it will not go well with the Christians, but if I tell them this, I will be considered a fool. On the other hand, if I remain silent, I shan't escape my conscience."[5]

Illuminato responded that Francis should rate God's opinion more highly than men's. So Francis sought an audience with Pelagius and told him of his vision. As Francis had feared, Pelagius merely scoffed and proceeded with his plans.

On August 29 the crusaders launched their attack. Most historians agree that five thousand crusaders died that day while at least one thousand were taken prisoner. Among those, fifty knights were summarily beheaded. The disaster could have been worse, for the crusaders were in panicked retreat with the Saracens hard on their trail, heading for the crusader camp. King John, now seventy years old, turned his men around and charged full tilt into the enemy, bringing his huge sword down like an executioner's ax right and left.

While the soldiers were recovering from their massive defeat, Francis made his move to end the fighting his own way.

He informed Cardinal Pelagius of his intention to cross enemy lines and seek a meeting with the sultan. Believing that such a move would mean certain death for the ignorant and misguided friar, the cardinal denied his request. Sir Steven Runciman in his three-volume history of the crusades had similar thoughts concerning Francis: "He had come to the East believing, as many other good and unwise persons before and after him had believed, that a peace mission can bring about peace."[6]

Francis left the camp anyway, along with the strapping Brother Illuminato, and headed directly to the camp of the Saracens. They took the same route as the crusaders had taken on the way to their crushing defeat. Years after their encounter with the sultan, Illuminato told Saint Bonaventure that, as he and Francis were walking, they chanted, "Though I walk through the valley of the shadow of death, I will fear no evil: for thou art with me" (Psalm 23:4 KJV). When they saw two lambs, Francis quoted the words of Jesus, "I send you out like sheep among wolves; be wary as serpents and innocent as doves . . . for men will hand you over to their courts; they will flog you . . . and you will be brought before governors and kings for my sake" (Matt. 10:16–18 NEB).

When they arrived at the Saracen stronghold, which was called Fariskur al-kamil, Thomas says that they were beaten by the sultan's soldiers. Runciman, on the other hand, writes that "the Muslim guards were suspicious at first but soon decided that anyone so simple, so gentle and so dirty must be mad, and treated him with the respect due to a man who had been touched by God."[7]

Francis was eventually taken before the sultan, who asked him if he was a messenger or if he wanted to become a Muslim.

Francis explained that he was the former, here to save the sultan's soul. Having learned some of the Muslim conventions before coming, Francis told the sultan to summon his religious advisers, since he knew that the sultan could not listen to a Christian unless they were with him.

The sultan's holy men decided to arrange a trap. The sultan held audience in an open space under canopies with silk cushions strewn around him. His spiritual advisers set an ornate carpet with crosses woven into its design in front of Francis, believing that he would be dishonoring Christ if he stepped on the crosses. They also knew that if he didn't approach the sultan, he would be insulting him. It was supposed to be a no-win proposition, but Francis, without hesitation, walked across the carpet and up to the sultan. When the holy men reproached him for his sacrilege, he replied that he had performed no sacrilege because Christians carried Christ's cross in their hearts.

His holy men insisted that the sultan should have the friars beheaded immediately. The sultan declined. For several days, Francis preached to the sultan, trying to convince him to accept Christ. Thomas says that the sultan was deeply moved by his words,[8] but apparently not enough to accept conversion.

Finally Francis issued a challenge to the sultan. Borrowing from the story of Elijah and the priests of Baal in the Old Testament, he said, "If you are afraid to abandon the law of Mahomet for Christ's sake, then light a big fire and I will go into it along with your priests. That will show you which faith is surer and more holy."

The sultan replied, perhaps with a grin, that none of his priests would want to expose themselves to the flames. Francis continued, "If you are prepared to promise me that you and your people will embrace the Christian religion if I come out of the fire unharmed, I will enter it alone. But if I am burned, you must attribute it to my sins; on the other hand, if God saves me by his power, you must acknowledge 'Christ the power of God, Christ the wisdom of God . . . as true God, the Lord and Savior of all.'"[9] The sultan respectfully declined.

Before Francis left, the sultan gave him many gifts. Thomas says that the sultan was surprised and admired Francis when he saw that Francis "despised" such things.

Francis returned to the crusader camp disappointed by his failure to win over the sultan and end the war. In September, the brothers arrived to join Francis—some from Assisi as well as Elias with the Syrian friars and a new German brother named Caesar. By then, however, Francis had fallen ill.

In October the sultan sent two captured knights to the crusader base with an offer: the Ayyubids would cede the whole of Palestine, except for the land beyond Jordan, in return for the invaders' withdrawal from Egypt. King John, the French, the Germans, and the English all favored the offer. Pelagius, the military orders, and the Italians, however, did not.

Finally on November 4, 1219, King John decided to end the long siege and take Damietta. In a driving thunderstorm they scaled the walls, captured a bastion, and smashed or burned their way through the gates. But what they found inside caused them to freeze in their tracks. The long siege had been more devastating than they had expected. Eighty thousand were dead, with only three thousand emaciated people left alive and only a hundred or fewer among them possessing the strength to offer a meager resistance. Even the hardened mercenaries were stunned at first, but then the long-frustrated crusaders burst into a rage, sacking the city, beating and raping the inhabitants, and taking many more off as slaves.

No record tells what Francis did between the occupation of Damietta and his appearance at Acre the following summer. He is believed to have sailed back to Acre with King John in February of 1220. We do know that King John was very impressed with Francis. He attended his canonization and, just before he died, was received into the third order.

About two years after Francis returned to Italy, Pelagius in Damietta rejected another peace offer from al-Kamil. He asked King John to return and lead an advance on Cairo. They were defeated and Pelagius was forced to capitulate. On September 8, 1222, the last crusader sailed away from Damietta.

While in Acre, Francis learned that five of the six brothers he had seen off to Morocco had been martyred there in January. Like successive blows from a heavy hammer more bad news followed. A young friar named Stephen arrived with word that rumors of Francis's death were wreaking havoc throughout the order. The newer friars had taken his reported demise as an opportunity to urge his vicars to ease up on the rules. At the Pentecost chapter the two vicars Francis had left behind had passed measures relaxing the rules about poverty. At the same time Cardinal Ugolino, while traveling to Perugia, had decided to impose the rule of Saint Benedict on several groups of the "poor sisters." Francis gathered his companions, Peter, Stephen, Elias, and Caesar, and wasted no time in arranging passage on the first available ship leaving Acre for Italy. It was a Venetian galley bound for Venice.

DIVISIONS AND REPERCUSSIONS

The divisiveness raging throughout the order was like a storm in Francis's soul. During the voyage to Venice, he learned that his vicars, Matthew and Gregory, had removed "take nothing with you" from the rules. The friars also wanted to ease the dietary regime—the frequency of fasts and the abstention from meat or other foods, remodeling it to resemble the less-demanding rules set up by monastic asceticism.

It soon became apparent that Ugolino's nephew, Gregory, was responsible for instigating many of the reforms now dividing the first order. He had also encouraged friars to set up buildings and libraries and to emulate the Benedictines and Cluniacs.

Francis and his four companions, Peter, Stephen, Elias, and Caesar, disembarked at the port in Venice. It was the busiest of ports, for, at that time, Venice was one of the world's most powerful states. But Francis didn't feel like hustle and bustle; he wanted a place of solitude. He left, perhaps with one companion, found a small boat, and rowed out to a little island in the lagoon. There, with the water lapping at the shore and gently rocking his boat, he prayed. With an anguished heart beneath the canopy of stars, he received a vision. He saw a small black hen surrounded by chicks that were skittering this way and that. There were so many that the little hen could not keep up with them. Francis interpreted the hen as being himself and decided that he needed an audience with the pope.[1]

Francis traveled from Venice, stopping in Verona and planning a stop in Bologna. But as he approached Bologna, he was horrified to hear that the friars were occupying a comfortable house filled with books. The house had even been given a name: "The brothers' house." Francis refused to go into the city but sent word ordering the brothers to vacate the house immediately.[2] They did so, but it was clear that things had gotten out of hand, just like they had with the hen who couldn't keep up with her chicks. Even more anxious to clean up this mess, Francis decided to bypass Assisi and go directly to Orvieto, about sixty-five miles southwest of Assisi, where Pope Honorius had set up court. He finally arrived there panting with urgency in August of 1220.

The vision of a hen that could not protect its chicks had prompted Francis to seek protection from the church, "who would use the rod to protect his Order from those of ill will." Francis kneeled before Pope Honorius and asked that he appoint a kind of second-level pope to watch over the brothers.

It was not only the divisiveness within the order that concerned Francis. News of the martyrdom of those friars in Morocco had been devastating. While the friars were finding more acceptance in Italy, many of them, especially those who crossed the Alps or the Mediterranean, entered regions where their order was unknown. Thought to be Albigensians or members of some other heretical group, they were being subjected to persecution from both laypeople and clergy.

In response to the issues Francis brought to his attention, the pope was determined to enforce the decrees of the Lateran council and acknowledge the canonical status of the order in a formal papal document. To deal with the divisive elements, he introduced a requirement that all applicants would undergo a full year's novitiate before their final acceptance.

With regard to his request for a secondary pope, Francis asked the pontiff to give the Lord Bishop Ugolino of Ostia power to oversee the affairs of the friars. Given his part and especially that of his nephew in making some of the unwanted reforms in the order, this seems a strange choice. It is even tempting to question whether the ease with which he granted Francis permission to visit the Holy Land was prompted by a desire to invoke reforms during his absence. But Francis had known and respected the cardinal bishop for some time and apparently believed he could win the support of this powerful man. Honorius granted his request, promising Francis his full support.

The Poverello left the pope and immediately sought out Bishop Ugolino. The bishop received him kindly and listened to his concerns. Seeing the fire in Francis's demeanor, he "was, from that moment, knit with the soul of Francis" and offered his protection in any way he could give it. Francis was so moved by the bishop's devotion that he fell at his feet and "entrusted himself and his brothers to him with a devout mind."[3]

He remained with the bishop, discussing the persecutions

that were plaguing the brothers in the north and the changes within the order that had been made during his absence. Ugolino agreed that the two vicars should be posted elsewhere and their changes summarily quashed. He also granted Francis his wish to stand down as head of the order in favor of Peter of Catania.

Francis was always jealous of any time that took him away from communion with his Lord. Consequently it was not difficult for him to turn over much of the busy work of the order to Peter and Ugolino. He was little interested in the details of organization and sought to remove himself from all cares and anxieties in order to seek solitude where "only the wall of the flesh would stand between him and God."[4]

A brother asked Francis why he was not, himself, fighting against the deviations and revisions from the rule. Francis responded, "My duty, my mandate as superior of the brothers, is of a spiritual order . . . If, through my exhortations and my example, I can neither suppress nor correct them, I do not wish to become an executioner who punishes and flogs, as the secular arm does. . . . Nevertheless, until the day of my death, I will continue to teach my brothers by my example and my life how to walk the road that the Lord showed me."[5]

Ugolino's role was built into the organizational structure of the order: Anyone who was not performing the office according to the rule and who wished to change it or who was not Catholic was to be presented to the *custos* [who played something of a "Sergeant of Arms" role] nearest to where He had been found. He was to guard him like a prisoner until the man could be turned over to his minister. That minister was to also watch over him like a prisoner until he could present this brother to the Lord of Ostia, who was now master protector and corrector of this brotherhood.[6]

The bishop, joined by several other cardinals, also began a campaign to send letters and prelates to the districts where the brothers were being persecuted. Peter of Catania, to whom Francis had turned over the position of minister general, died unexpectedly in March of 1222. Elias was appointed to take his place. The friars also learned that Honorius had granted canonical status to the "third order" of penitents.

Francis continued to be troubled by internal controversies as if they were a plague of flies. He cursed those in the order who were clothed with three instead of the allowed two garments or who, without necessity, wore fine, soft garments. Such activity, he said, indicated an "extinguished spirit."[7] Once, before a chapter was due to be held at Portiuncula, the people of Assisi became concerned that, given the increasing size of the order, there was no house large enough in which the brothers could adequately meet. Without asking Francis and perhaps in hopes of offering him a delightful surprise, they built a house. Francis was upset when he returned to Portiuncula and saw the new building. The brothers were allowed to live only in the most ramshackle lodgings and were, by no means, to own anything. This building did not fulfill the code of poverty set by Francis. Finding an obvious breach of the rule right here at the hub of the order was too much for him. Deeply incensed, he leaped onto the building and climbed up to the roof, where he began ripping out the tiles and tossing them off to the ground.

Some of the men from Assisi happened by and were distressed that what they had undertaken with a spirit of charity was being so ill treated. They explained to Francis that the building belonged to the city and was a gift for the friars to use. No doubt ashamed of his outburst, he climbed down from the roof with a contrite heart.

The depth of his displeasure was revealed one day while he was suffering physically. He forced himself up on his couch and said to those who were caring for him, "Who are these who have snatched my order and that of my brothers out of my hands? If I go to the general chapter, I will show them what my will is."[8] How far he was willing to go to enforce his will would soon be revealed at the Pentecost chapter of 1222.

The growth of the order was clearly displayed on that day when about five thousand friars from all over Europe, along with hordes of laypeople, assembled around the little chapel at Portiuncula. Every day that week Ugolino rode over with an imposing escort of churchmen, counts, lords, knights, and gentlemen. When he came, all the brothers would process out to meet him. He would dismount from his horse and walk back with them to Santa Maria, where he would preach.

The tents in the encampment were made of willow-trellis and of rush matting and assigned to groups from each province. As a result, the chapter of 1222 became called "the Chapter of the trellises." The brothers in attendance, of course, had neither tables nor chairs, but the people from Assisi and the surrounding areas provided for them generously. A passage from *Little Flowers* describes the event. "The inhabitants of Perugia, Spoleto, Foligno, Spello, Assisi and its neighborhood arrived with pack animals and carts laden with bread and beans, cheese, wine, and other good things. They also brought enough table cloths, dishes, bowls, pitchers and glasses for the entire company, vying with each other to serve the friars."[9] It was a noisy but festive crowd—an amazing tribute of the love the people now held for Francis and the friars.

The climax of the chapter of 1222 came when some of the ministers and priests persuaded the cardinal to again ask Francis to adopt a less demanding pattern of regular life. Francis listened as the cardinal bishop presented their case. Afterward he took the hand of Ugolino and walked through the crowd of friars until he stood before them, still holding the hand of the bishop.

He then said, "My brothers, my brothers! God has called me to follow the way of simplicity, and I don't want you to continue pressing some other rule on me—neither St. Augustine's nor St. Bernard's, nor St. Benedict's. The Lord told me he wished me to be a new kind of fool and doesn't want us to be guided by any higher learning than that. God will confound you for your knowledge and sagacity and I trust that his constables will punish you for them. Then, to your shame, you will return to your first state." Ugolino was dumfounded and said nothing. The friars were suddenly filled with fear.[10]

In spite of the controversy, Francis's fame continued to grow. On August 15, 1222, he went to Bologna for the Feast of the Assumption and was asked to speak. Years later a priest called Thomas, then Archdeacon of Spalato in Dalmatia, wrote, "When I was a student in Bologna I saw St. Francis preach in the main square outside the Palazzo Communal; almost the whole city had gathered to hear him. His theme was 'Angels, Men and Devils.' . . . He wore a tattered habit, his appearance was insignificant, and his face wasn't handsome; but God gave his words such power that they actually restored peace to many of the noble families long torn apart by hatred, cruelty and murder. At the same time ordinary men and women flocked to him out of devotion and respect, afterwards trying to tear a shred from his habit or at least to touch him."[11]

Francis continued to resist changes in the order. He persisted in arguing against books and education, but on this issue Ugolino could not agree with him. A well-educated man himself who highly valued learning, he insisted that Francis reopen the house in Bologna. Francis finally relented, but insisted that it must not be owned by the friars. Ugolino paid for the friars' books and the materials for their studies out of his own funds.

There were times when Francis tried to be more open-minded about the various issues. A friar came to him once and asked him about what he could wear. Francis shrugged and reluctantly told the friar that he could do whatever his minister said. Moments later he ran after the friar. With his usual flair for the dramatic, he told the young man to "come back and show me the place where I said that." When they reached that place, Francis said, "I was wrong brother. I was wrong. Whoever wishes to be a Friar Minor should have nothing except a tunic as the Rule allows, with a cord and breeches."[12]

In response to the turmoil within the order, Francis began writing a new rule. He was working on it when he traveled to Rome in the winter of 1222. Whenever he was in Rome, he retreated to a secluded church or to his cell in the retreat house that Giacoma de Settesoli had set up for the order. She had been giving generously to the third order, which was growing nicely. He was particularly pleased when she would bring him a favorite treat. It was one of Giacoma's specialties—a little almond cake called mostacciuoli.

Francis had been planning to go on north to Fonte Colombo to finish writing his rule, but one of his admirers, Cardinal Leo Brancaleone of the Holy Cross in Rome, offered him a place to stay before he left. He had tried to anticipate the Poverello's peculiar needs and arranged a place in one of the unoccupied towers of his palace. The rooms were virtually bare, which he thought would offer the kind of stark living in which Francis would feel comfortable. He even offered him a group of paupers to eat with. In addition, Angelo di Tancredi, who was temporarily acting as the cardinal's chaplain, would look after him.

That night, however, Francis said that he was "attacked and beaten by devils." Afterward, "trembling and shaking . . . like a person suffering a severe fever," he called to Angelo, who was sleeping in another vault, and asked him to stay with him.

Francis always said that angels "act as our guardians" and "walk in the midst of the shadow of death with us." However, on this occasion he thought the devils were acting as "officers of our Lord." Even with the sparse conditions in the tower, Francis felt guilty for staying in such a palatial home. He believed this provided a bad example for the brothers who were living in poverty. The attack he therefore regarded as punishment for his indiscretion. The next morning he went to the cardinal, told him everything that had happened, and then left.[13]

Francis was feeling ill by the time he left Rome. Rain continued to pour down as he made his way toward Terni. When he reached there, the weather had calmed enough for him to preach in the square. A bishop in attendance told him that God always sent holy men to enrich the church's life, but in Francis, he had sent a "lowly and uneducated little man to bring it luster."

Francis moved on until he came to the Rieti valley, where he joined Leo, Angelo, and Rufino at the hermitage Fonte Colombo. He had also brought a canon lawyer to help him finish the rule. On its woodland heights, the location is watered by a spring and provides a magnificent view across the valley to the snowy summit of Mount Terminillo. Francis settled near a little chapel dedicated to Saint Mary Magdalene. The steps behind the chapel lead down a cliff face, first to Leo's cave and then, below it, to a curving fissure created by an earthquake. Francis lived and worked there with his canon lawyer for the next six weeks.

While at Fonte Colombo, Francis was again bothered by devils. The morning after the attack his companions found him prostrate before the altar. Leo prayed fervently and was caught up in a vision. He saw among the many thrones in heaven one that was "more honorable than the rest, ornamented with precious stones, and radiant with all glory." He wondered who it belonged to and then heard a voice saying that it had belonged to one of the fallen angels. It was now reserved for "the humble Francis."

Leo later asked Francis what he thought of himself and Francis answered that he was the "greatest of sinners." The Holy Spirit then spoke to Leo confirming that his vision was true, "for humility will raise this most humble man to the throne that was lost through pride."[14]

The fact that Francis was working on the new rule was widely known. Several ministers, fearing that Francis's new rule would still be too difficult, asked Elias, who was respected for his negotiating skills, to accompany a delegation to Francis and help present their case.

When the delegation arrived and Elias presented their ultimatum, Francis raised his eyes toward heaven and said, "Lord, didn't I tell you that they wouldn't believe you."

Leo attested that "the voice of Christ was heard in the air replying, 'Francis there is nothing of yours in the Rule; it is all mine. I want the Rule to be observed to the letter, to the letter, to the letter, and without gloss, without gloss, without gloss.'" Francis turned and asked the ministers if they had heard the voice. They said that they hadn't and left in confusion.

Although hurt by the betrayal of the rebellious ministers, Francis perceived the need to make some concessions in an effort to restore unity. Francis's second rule that he fashioned in the cave is harsher than the first in the punishments designed for those breaking the rule. On the other hand, his new rule was more relaxed in omitting the commands to "carry nothing for your journey" and to "offering no resistance to violence." It also permitted wearing working shoes and ownership of a breviary.

The general chapter endorsed this new version of the rule at Pentecost. Francis then went to Rome, where Cardinal Ugolino took him to see the pope. Pope Honorius approved the second rule in his *Bull Sole Anmuere* in November of 1223.

After the next chapter the brothers were sent to the provinces equipped with the letters and with the new rule containing the seal of the pope.

MIRACLES IN THE SHADOW OF DEATH

Winter had once more closed about Umbria. The air was crisp and held a feeling like Christmas. Of all the hermitages in the Rieti Valley, Greccio was Francis's favorite. Most of the local inhabitants had joined his order of penitents. Woods on the hillsides were populated by deer, foxes, and an occasional family of wild boars or wolves. The hermitage clung to a cliff under the cover of trees, which leaned over the crest.

It was three years before his death and Francis had scenes of the nativity on his mind. An idea began to form in his theatrical imagination. He had a special friend in Greccio named Giovanni who had been born noble. He sent for Giovanni about fifteen days before Christmas and asked him to prepare a nativity scene.

With the pope's permission and Giovanni di Velita's help, the people built and stocked a stable near the hermitage. On Christmas Eve, when darkness fell, the friars around the valley joined a long procession of families climbing up to it. People came as they could with candles and torches to light up the night, and there was singing, praising, and a celebration of the mass.

Francis appeared in the nativity scene dressed like a deacon, which he was, and called Jesus the "Child of Bethlehem."[1]

Thomas waxed eloquent about the event:

> Simplicity is honored there, poverty is exalted, humility is commended and a new Bethlehem, as it were, is made from Greccio. Night is illuminated like the day, delighting men and beasts. The people come and joyfully celebrate the new mystery. The forest resounds with voices and the rocks respond to their rejoicing. The brothers sing, discharging their debt of praise to the Lord, and the whole night echoes with jubilation. The holy man of God stands before the manger full of sighs, consumed by devotion and filled with a marvelous joy. The solemnities of the mass are performed over the manger, and the priest experiences a new consolation.[2]

A man had a vision while participating in the ceremony. He told of seeing the baby dead in the manger but the babe awoke when Francis picked it up. This was said to refer to the fact that "the Child Jesus had been forgotten in the hearts of many." The continued tradition of creating a nativity scene each year is attributed to Francis and that night in Greccio. The hay from the scene was kept and used, which reportedly led to many animals being healed of illnesses.

In 1224, Francis, now forty-three years old, left the Spoleto valley to go into Romagna with Brother Leo. Along the way they passed the foot of the castle of Montefeltro. They could hear that a great celebration was in progress. Francis learned that they were celebrating the recent granting of knighthood to one of the counts of Montefeltro. They climbed the road up to the castle, passed through the gate, and joined a huge crowd of people. Flags and banners were tagging the wind while jugglers and acrobats performed.

One of the nobles present was a wealthy and powerful gentleman from Tuscany, Orlando di Chiusi of Casentino. Having heard many great things about Francis, he deeply venerated him and wanted to see and hear him preach. Francis therefore passed through the crowded courtyard, jostling the shoulders of the noble men and women and gentlemen. Then he mounted a parapet and began to preach. He chose for the text of his sermon these words: "So great is the good that I hope for, that all pain delights me." Leo writes that he spoke on this theme "by the dictation of the Holy Spirit so fervently and profoundly, citing the divers pains and sufferings of the holy apostles and holy martyrs and the severe penances of holy confessors and the manifold tribulations and temptations of holy virgins and other saints, that all the people stood with their eyes and their minds turned towards him, and listened as if an angel of God spoke." It is not difficult to wonder if this was a presage of the sufferings ahead for Francis. Count Orlando was so moved by Francis's preaching that he gave him the use of a mountain in the Rieti valley at La Verna.[3]

A few months later the hermitage established there was to have a singular destiny. Weary of the crowds, Francis began to long for a time and place of solitude where he could devote himself to prayer and to communing with God. In August, he decided to precede the feast of Saint Michael with a forty-day fast at the new hermitage in La Verna. His health was now, without question, failing. While in the Holy Land, he had picked up what most physicians now believe to have been trachoma. It was getting worse, and light striking his eyes was getting so painful that he often had to cover his face with his hood. He was so ill that Leo, Angelo, and Masseo, who came along to protect him,[4] convinced a peasant to lend him a donkey so that he wouldn't have to walk. When the peasant handed him the reins, he asked, "Are you Francis of Assisi himself?" After getting his answer the peasant said, "Well, then, try to be as good as you can, because everyone has great faith in you and you mustn't let them down." Francis was so touched with the man's simple words that he dismounted and kissed his feet.[5]

The peasant's donkey succeeded in getting Francis to La Verna. The retreat, which they named Isola Maggiore, was a small island on Lake Trasimene, west of Perugia. Francis found shelter at night under the pines in a hollow of brambles overlooking the water. The site has a history that is a counterpoint to its beauty, for beneath the water were still the bones of the Roman army that was caught by surprise and massacred by the Carthaginians under Hannibal in 217 BC. Now, it was a very tranquil setting, animated only by lizards, salamanders, and butterflies, the rich greenery highlighted by the purple herons and white egrets that fished the reed beds, as described by Adrian House.

The setting is dramatic. Cliff faces jut from the earth as if only recently thrust up by primeval forces. Contorted rocks intrude upon walking spaces, giving an impression of cataclysmic conflict. An enormous ledge called the Sasso Spicco juts out horizontally from the cliff, serving as a roof to the gallery where Francis usually prayed.

Francis was forever trying to learn how he might most perfectly conform to the will of God. As he said of the apostles and martyrs in his sermon to the nobles, he was willing to endure every bodily torment and every mental distress if only "the will of the Father in heaven might be mercifully fulfilled in [him]."[6]

Francis prayed fervently the entire time he was at La Verna. Once he took the Bible and opened it to a place where it spoke of the passion of Jesus. The essence of it was an affirmation that Jesus would suffer much tribulation. Francis opened the Bible two more times to make sure that he had not opened to this passage by chance. But after doing so he was convinced that he, Francis, was to suffer much tribulation as well before his death.

While at La Verna, Francis had a vision of a man standing or hovering above him. He had many wings like a seraph, but his hands were extended and his feet joined together. Then Francis noticed that he was fixed to a cross. Two of the wings were extended above his head; two were stretched out to each side as if for flight; and two more were wrapped around his body. Francis looked at the seraph's face and, although he had never seen Jesus physically face to face, believed that his "features were clearly those of the Lord Jesus."

The seraph, whose beauty Francis described as "being beyond estimation," gave Francis a "kind and gracious look." However, the seraph was nailed to the cross and Francis could see that he was suffering pain. Then the vision faded.

While Francis was trying to understand what the vision of the seraph meant, something incredible began happening to him:

the marks of nails began to form on his own hands and feet!

Thomas of Celano describes the wounds in great detail. "His hands and feet seemed to be pierced through the middle by nails, with the heads of the nails appearing in the inner side of the hands and on the upper sides of the feet and their pointed ends on the opposite sides." The marks "on the outer side" of the hands where the nails would have emerged from the flesh looked like "the ends of the nails, bent and driven back." "The marks of the nails" on the feet had a similar appearance. "Furthermore, his right side was as though it had been pierced by a lance and had a wound in it that frequently bled so that his tunic and trousers were very often covered with his sacred blood."[7]

Thomas writes that Francis had these five signs "as though he had hung upon the cross with the Son of God." What made this happening even more incredible at the time is that it *had never happened before* in the recorded history of the church! Twelve centuries had passed since the death of Jesus, and this was the first time anyone had experienced the stigmata. Given the deep humility that he always tried to maintain, it is not surprising that Francis made no mention of the wounds and, in fact, tried to keep them secret.

What exactly happened to Francis at La Verna is, of course, subject to interpretation. For the faithful, Francis experienced a great miracle, a testament in his body, as it were, of his life given to seeking and communing with Christ. Other explanations, of course, have been offered. Chiara Frugoni, the author of a recent biography on Francis, points out that his health had been failing long before he came to La Verna. He was already covered with sores and ulcers that bled frequently, and he suffered recurrent bouts of fever from malaria. Because of his heavy ministry to lepers, he might have contracted a form of leprosy, and this could have caused the sores on his body to resemble the heads of nails.

Though extremely ill, Francis left Sasso Spicco the morning after Saint Michael's Day in August of 1224. He and his companions rode down into the Rieti valley and spent the night at Monte-Casale, a little hermitage above Borgo San Sepolcro. When he decided to remain there a few days, he sent the horse loaned to him by Count Orlando back to La Verna via one of the friars. This is when the miracle for the woman who had been so long in labor was supposed to have occurred.

The friars at Borgo San Sepolcro had been troubled by robbers who, when bereft of other victims, had been targeting them as their last resort. Francis told the brothers to go the extra mile—to take bread, wine, cheese, eggs, plates, and glasses to them. While the robbers were enjoying their meal, the friars asked why they led such dangerous lives when they could live off the land. The gang began bringing firewood to the friary and three eventually joined them.

After spending a few days there, Francis and his companions moved on to Citta di Castello, where they remained for about a month. They then moved on to Assisi, but winter had begun to set and they were forced to spend the night under a rock with snow whirling around them. Finally they made it to Portiuncula, but Francis turned it into merely a pit stop in Assisi before pressing on to preach at more towns in southern Umbria.[8]

By the time he returned to Portiuncula the second time, the pain in his eyes was driving him to flee from light. Elias revived his efforts to convince the Poverello to seek medical treatment.

Francis had consistently resisted the aid of doctors; he wanted only "to depart and to be with Christ." Actually, Francis had little regard for healing because he had so little regard for the body. He considered the body to be the "enemy of the soul." In his first rule, he wrote that a brother who becomes upset trying to save his body with remedies is acting from evil and the flesh "because he loves his body more than his soul." Brother Elias persisted until he finally convinced Francis to seek medical help for his eyes. Francis, however, managed to put him off for a time in order to rest.

Francis chose to spend that time close to Clare and the "poor ladies." Now, almost blind and virtually helpless, the pain forced him to flee light so that his rest was taken in a little darkened cell. It was the kind of circumstance that made a man easy prey for discouragement and depression. Every day he spent hours weeping "tears of penitence," as memories of his early years coursed through his mind.

It would have been difficult, with Francis so close and so helpless, for Clare to remain away from him. But his own rules regarding interaction with women were so strict, and he was always so concerned about his example for the brothers, that we would expect Francis to reject her attention. Perhaps, though, amid suffering and sadness, he may have, for once, allowed her to have her way.

Some reports indicate that she was indeed with him during this time, often seated at his feet. At first she made him a large cell of reeds in the monastery garden, where he would be able to move about freely. Unfortunately, the pleasant little nest became infested with rats and mice, which constantly ran across his bed. He finally moved into a hut outside the convent.

In the meantime Francis did as he always did and bared his soul to God. His spirits began to rise when he received assurance from the Lord that he would enjoy heavenly glory. The sisters began hearing him sing songs from his resting place. His smile returned and one day after a meal, while he was sitting in the deep shade with Clare at the monastery table, he suddenly had a distant look that transformed into ecstasy. Although engulfed with darkness and pain, Francis wrote *The Canticle of Brother Sun*.

Most high, all-powerful, all good, Lord!
All praise is yours, all glory, all honor
And all blessing.
To you, alone, Most High, do they belong,
No mortal lips are worthy
To pronounce your name.
All praise be yours, my Lord, through all that you have made,
And first my lord Brother Sun,
Who brings the day; and light you give to us through him,
How beautiful is he, how radiant in all his splendor!
Of you, Most High, he bears the likeness.
All praise be yours, my Lord, through Sister Moon and Stars;
In the heavens you have made them, bright
And precious and fair.
All praise be yours, my Lord, through Brothers Wind and Air,
And fair and stormy, all the weather's moods,
By which you cherish all that you have made.
All praise be yours, my Lord, through Sister Water,
So useful, lowly, precious and pure,
All praise be yours, my Lord, through Brother Fire,

Through whom you brighten up the night.
How beautiful is he, how gay! Full of power and strength.
All praise be yours, my Lord, through Sister Earth, our mother,
Who feeds us in her sovereignty and produces
Various fruits with colored flowers and herbs.
Praise and bless my Lord, and give him thanks,
And serve him with great humility.[9]

The beauty and ecstasy of this celebrated song was at first eclipsed by signs of political and social turmoil throughout the region. The struggle between the Perugian people and the knights of the city had broken out twice since 1214: in 1217 and in 1222, the last happening after Francis prophesied that it was coming the day the knights of Perugia had engaged in training exercises in the piazza where Francis was trying to preach.

Assisi had taken advantage of this recurring conflict and, during each outbreak, had extended its holdings to nearby cities. When the knights were defeated in the outbreak of 1222, they came to Assisi, asking for the city's support. A pact to that effect was drawn up and signed in 1223. Less than two years later, in the late spring of 1225, civil war raged in Perugia again and the cost in destruction and the shedding of blood was great. Trying to resolve the conflict, the pope tried to sever Assisi's involvement and dissolved the treaty. The podesta of Assisi, Oportulo di Bernardo, pledged to keep the agreement and led the communal army in support of the Perugian knights.

Bishop Guido, Francis's old friend, excommunicated the podesta for openly challenging the pope. The podesta, furious at the actions of the bishop, struck back at him by placing an economic blockade against the bishop's palace. The conflict spread through the city, causing factions to rise against each other in bloody reprisals.

Troubled by what he heard, Francis's concern was amplified by the fact that both men were strong friends and supporters—the bishop, all the way back to his conversion, and the podesta by virtue of the fact that his daughter, Agnes, had joined Clare at San Damiano.

Francis added another verse to his canticle of the sun. He then called in one of his companions and sent him with a message to the podesta. It said that he, along with any other officials he could bring with him, was to go to the bishop's palace. Francis then called still more friars and told them to go to the bishop's house and sing *The Canticle of the Sun*. The verse he added goes,

> All praise be yours, my Lord, through those who grant pardon
> For love of you; through those who endure
> Sickness and trial
> Happy those who endure in peace,
> By you, Most High, they will be crowned.

The faces of the two adversaries were still hard and twisted with anger when the friars began to sing the canticle, but when they came to the newly added last verse, the podesta broke into tears. When he recovered, he apologized to the bishop and kneeled down before him. In a similar response the bishop took the podesta's hands and raised him back up, apologizing for the anger that was his weakness.

Francis ended up staying at San Damiano much longer than

he had promised—from the end of July to the beginning of September, 1225, and Elias was anxious to get him to Rieti, where he knew of a doctor who came highly recommended.

They were surprised to discover the Roman curia lodged there, including Pope Honorius and Bishop Ugolino. Conflict between pope and emperor and rebellion in Rome were frequent occurrences. Honorius had been forced to leave Rome in April of 1225, first going to Tivoli and then to Rieti, and would not return until the end of 1226. Many doctors had come to Rieti, in fact, to be of service to the pope.

During the days when he was having eye treatments in Rieti, Francis spent most of the time in his nearby hermitage, where Angelo, Rufino, Leo, and Masseo attended to his daily needs. Once while there, he asked a companion who had been a lute player to play for him. The companion, being a conscientious friar, declined, fearing that someone might suspect him of engaging in frivolity. Francis understood his reticence and dropped the issue, but the next night, while Francis was meditating, he heard the sound of a lute playing. It was so beautiful that he thought "he was being translated to another world."[10]

Doctors in Italy at the time wore red robes. Because of the expensive red pigment and the trimming made of vair, a highly prized fur, they were very costly. Two procedures formed the basis of medical treatment: checking the patient's pulse and examining the patient's urine against the light. While at the hermitage, Francis invited the doctor who was treating his eyes to come to dinner. But when he told his brothers of the upcoming visit, they were distressed because they were so poor and could offer little to eat. The doctor happened to be outside and overheard them.

When they opened the door, he kindly responded that he would consider their poverty to be a real delicacy. To everyone's delight and amazement, a woman came to the door soon thereafter with a basket of food that included bread, fish, lobster pies, honey, and grapes. She handed it to them, accepted their thanks, and left.

A doctor in Rieti, referred to as Master Nichola, recommended a radical treatment for Francis's eyes that consisted of cauterizing the veins in the temple. He believed that this procedure, while painful, would stem the flow of tears and pus in his eyes. Francis reluctantly acquiesced. The brazier was lit and Master Nichola plunged his branding irons into it until they glowed red hot. At that point, while the other brothers were transfixed with horror, Francis said to the fire, "My brother fire that surpasses all other things in beauty, the Most High created you strong, beautiful and useful. Be kind to me in this hour; be courteous, for I have loved you in the past in the Lord. I beg our Creator, who made you, to temper your heat so that I can bear it."

His companions slipped out, unable to stand watching their spiritual father subjected to such pain. But when they returned they saw the doctor standing beside Francis in amazement. Francis had apparently not felt a thing.

While undergoing treatment, Francis continued to make every effort to hide the stigmata. One person noticed the imprint in his feet and asked about it, but Francis essentially said, "Mind your own business."

He often washed only his fingers to keep observers from seeing the imprint on his hands. He used a similar process to wash his feet. When someone wanted to kiss his hand, he extended only his fingers and sometimes only his sleeve. His feet he covered with the woolen socks that Clare made for him.

Francis would cover the wound in his side with his hand when he took off his tunic for it to be washed. This action proved to be insufficient, for Rufino, who one day offered to clean his tunic, managed to discover it. Those few who did see the stigmata, and it is unclear if there were more than just Elias and Rufino, learned to avoid saying anything but to merely avert their eyes.

The operation and other treatments for his trachoma proved unsuccessful, and Francis decided that it was time to proceed to Assisi. He and his company bade farewell to Honorius and Ugolino and then headed on northward toward Assisi. Elias was not willing to give up on medical treatments, however, so he convinced Francis that they should go to Siena, which had some of Italy's finest doctors. Siena, however, was in Tuscany, well to the north, at least a difficult fifteen-day walk for someone in Francis's delicate condition. They stopped on the way to spend Lent and Easter at Greccio and then traveled on several more days to a friary just north of Siena. Having received word that Francis was coming, a large crowd gathered to welcome him. In spite of all their efforts, the physicians failed to make any progress. In fact, his health seemed to worsen and he spent one night vomiting blood.

Francis seemed so gravely ill that his companions believed the end to be near. They sent a message to Elias and waited for Francis to speak his last words. He said, "Since I cannot speak much because of my weakness and pain, I wish briefly to make my purpose clear to all my brothers present and to come. I wish them always to love one another as I have loved them; let them always love and honor our Lady Poverty and let them remain faithful and obedient to the bishops and clergy of holy mother church."[11]

After Elias arrived, Francis seemed to recover. Finally Francis insisted that they go home.

The group hurried toward Assisi, but, on the way, Francis suffered another relapse. His stomach, as well as his legs and feet, began to swell and he could hardly bear to eat, so they stopped at the hermitage of Le Celle in the hills outside Cortona.

Le Celle is nestled beside a stream in a steep gorge a few miles north of Lake Trasimeno. Some say that it is the most picturesque of all the early Franciscan retreats. From the top of the short trail down there is a sweeping view of the plain. The depth of the ravine is accentuated by tall green poplars and the dark shafts of the cypress trees that flank the sloping path. Biographer House writes: "At the bottom near the sanctuary, there is the smell of honeysuckle, roses, oregano and thyme and a deep silence broken only by the trickle of water and the songs of the blackbirds."[12]

When Francis became well enough to travel, they left Le Celle. By now, Francis's fame had grown so that his sainthood seemed inevitable. But the body of a saint in those days was valuable, even more so than the relics that everyone prized. It would attract pilgrims and travelers and could contribute much to the prosperity of a city. Given Assisi's persistent conflict with Perugia, the brothers feared that people from that city might try to steal Francis. Consequently, they detoured around Perugia, passing through the hills beside Gubbio until they came to a new hermitage in the hills at Bagnara, just outside of Nocera, about eighteen miles east of Assisi.

Early in September, Berlingerio, the podesta of Assisi,

received an urgent message saying that they needed his help to bring Francis home.

The people of Assisi were anxious for Francis's return. He had become the "glory of Assisi," and they wanted no other city to claim his body. The podesta therefore dispatched an escort of knights and burgesses, some of them probably Francis's friends from his playboy days, to carry him back to Assisi. Soon after dawn the armed cavalcade left with the Poverello and headed west through farmland, around the hilltop castle of Postignano, and then toward Mount Subasio.

On the way they needed provisions and entered a poor village named Satriano. They were, however, unable to find a place to buy food. Francis told them that they trusted more in their "flies" (his name for money) than in God. He then told them to go out into the village and ask for alms. They did so, albeit with a degree of embarrassment, and succeeded in finding enough sustenance to hold them over.

The final trek to Assisi was accompanied by flashes of lightning as the procession crossed beneath Mount Subasio. They climbed the road to the city, but as they passed through the great Sant'Antimo gate, the sky broke open and the procession continued under heavy rainfall. The brothers with him, and the people who had braved the clouds to greet their "Father," covered their heads and ran alongside, splashing through puddles and gathering a spattering of mud. The procession passed through the Piazza del Commune, past Francis's former home, and proceeded on to the bishop's palace. There, surrounded by splendor, Francis lay sick and blind, wearing a fur cap and a tunic of sackcloth and covered with a sackcloth blanket.

LAST DAYS

All praise be yours, my Lord, through Sister Death,
From whose embrace no mortal can escape.
Woe to those who die in mortal sin!
Happy those She finds doing your will!
For them the second death shall never harm.[1]

While lying in the bishop's palace, Francis added a final verse to his canticle, this one focused upon "Sister Death," whose approach he awaited.

Sometime later, when he was considering the divisions within the order, within maybe a month or so of his death, Francis wrote (or dictated to Leo) his *Testament*. He stressed that it was not a substitute for his rule that had been approved a few years earlier, but it did lay out some of the precepts of his life that he considered most important: prayer (including the office), poverty (which still forbade the ownership of property), humility, and obedience (including strict observance of the sacraments). It was less than a page in length, very succinct, but something that he may have hoped would be the final word on these issues and, without saying it, might be held binding for the friars.

Francis called in those brothers closest to him to bless them following the tradition of Jacob and Moses. As they gathered around the dying Francis, he spoke comforting words to them all. Then he extended his right hand toward them and said, "Farewell all you my sons, in the fear of the Lord." Then, placing his hand upon the head of each in turn, beginning with his vicar, he blessed them.

Francis crossed his right hand over his left in imitation of Jacob's blessing and placed his hand on Elias's head. He couldn't see, so he asked the others to confirm that it was indeed Elias. He blessed Elias, saying, "You, my son, I bless above all and throughout all, and, just as the Most High has multiplied my brothers and sons in your hands, so also I bless them all upon you and in you. May God, the kindest of all, bless you in heaven and upon earth." He concluded by saying, "May the Lord be mindful of your work and of your labor, and may a share be reserved for you in the reward of the just. May you find every blessing you desire, and may whatever you ask worthily be granted to you."[2]

Francis was never able to feel comfortable in a palace and finally asked the brothers to take him to Saint Mary of the Portiuncula. He said that he wanted "to give back his soul to God in that place where he first knew the way of truth perfectly."

Another procession carried Francis past his old school, at the Church of San Giorgio, through the Moiano gate, and down the road toward their old home. Francis had often reminded his brothers that they must never abandon the church of Saint Mary of the Portiuncula, for Francis thought it to be especially holy—"a dwelling place of God."[3] Portiuncula was now a friary with thatched huts surrounding his little chapel in the woods. After resting a few days by the church, he called in two brothers and gave them a particularly difficult assignment. They were to "sing in a loud voice with joy of spirit the Praises of the Lord" over his death. Death was coming; he knew it and he wanted to spend his last days there praising God and teaching his brothers how to praise God. He said that he welcomed his "Sister Death." Death to him was the gateway to life.

Francis asked that Lady Giacoma be summoned. A message was written, and a messenger made ready to deliver that message to Rome when she and her servants unexpectedly arrived. There was some hesitation to admit her, due to her sex, but Francis bid her to come in, saying "Brother Giacoma" did not have to observe the decree against women.

To everyone's surprise, she had brought what the unde-livered message had asked for: ashen-colored cloth, imported by the Cistercians, to cover his body; many candles; a cloth to cover his face, a little pillow on which to rest his head, and, of course, the sweet little almond cakes he loved so much.

After Giacoma prepared her confection for Francis, he remembered that Bernard had always loved them, too, and sent someone to fetch him. When Bernard came in, his face furrowed in sorrow, he sat next to the bed and made a request, "Father! I beg you, bless me and show me your love. I believe that, if you show me your love with fatherly affection, God Himself and the other brothers of the religion will love me more."[4]

Francis accidentally put his hand on the head of Giles instead of Bernard. Someone, probably Giles, moved his hand over to

Bernard, whom Francis proceeded to bless: "Brother Bernard was the first brother the Lord gave me. He began first and most perfectly fulfilled the perfection of the holy Gospel, distributing all his goods to the poor. Because of this and his many other prerogatives, I am bound to love him more than any other brother in the whole religion. As much as I am able, it is my will and command that whoever becomes general minister should love and honor him as he would me."[5]

The people of Assisi—commoners, merchants, gentlemen, and nobles—awaited his death with bated breath. Francis, who had always been slight of frame, was now little more than skin and bone, losing strength with every passing breath until he could hardly move. A brother asked if he would prefer to suffer from a long illness or endure the suffering of martyrdom. Francis responded, "My son, that has always been and still is most dear to me . . . which pleases the Lord my God . . . for I desire always only to be found conformed and obedient to his will in all things." But then he added, "Yet, this infirmity is harder for me to bear even for three days than any martyrdom."[6]

Elias remembered in silence what he had been told two years ago, while Francis and he were staying at Foligno. They were sleeping when a "white-garbed priest of a very great and advanced age and of venerable appearance" appeared standing before Brother Elias. The priest said to him, "Arise, Brother, and say to Brother Francis that eighteen years are now completed since he renounced the world and gave himself to Christ, and that he will remain in this life for only two more years; then the Lord will call him to himself and he will go the way of all flesh."[7] Elias wondered if his holy father remembered that vision.

A brother who was standing nearby said that, in losing him, they were losing their light and asked him for forgiveness and to extend his blessing to those not present. Francis answered, "Behold, my son, I am called by God; I forgive my brothers, both present and absent, all their offenses and faults, and, in as far as I am able, I absolve them; I want you to announce this to them and to bless them all on my behalf."

Francis asked that bread be brought to him; then he broke it and gave a piece of it to them all. He asked someone to read from the gospel of John: "It was just before the Passover Feast. Jesus knew that the time had come for him to leave this world and go to the Father. Having loved his own who were in the world, he now showed them the full extent of his love" (13:1).

Francis asked that later he be clothed in a hair shirt and sprinkled with ashes. Now, though, he wanted to be placed naked upon the bare ground so that he "could wrestle naked with a naked enemy." He asked the brothers to let him lie there after his death "for the time it takes one to walk a [mile] unhurriedly."

One of the brothers took the tunic and trousers and a little cap of sackcloth and said, perhaps with a hint of humor, "Know that this tunic and trousers and cap have been lent to you by me. . . . But that you may know that you have no ownership with regard to them, I take away from you all authority to give them to anyone." Francis's face slowly creased into a smile, as he realized he had "kept faith with Lady Poverty to the end." Years later that tunic would end up in the possession of the King of France.

There was a kind of vigil outside the church the night of Francis's death. Throughout the night the people of Assisi and large parties from neighboring towns and villages made their way to Santa Maria by the light of torches and flares. The crowd joined the friars in chanting praise and thanksgiving, holding up lights so that it looked like what Thomas described as "a wake of angels."[8]

Larks came to the roof of the house, though it was already twilight when they are normally at rest, and flew around the house several times making considerable noise. The city watchmen who guarded the place were amazed.

As the brothers inside placed Francis on the ground, he covered the wound in his right side with his left hand to keep it from being seen. He then said, "I have done what was mine to do; may Christ teach you what you are to do."[9] At the point of death Francis recited (or sang), with his last few breaths, the psalm of David, "I cried to the Lord with my voice; with my voice I made supplication to the Lord." Hardly a breath could be heard, and as their eyes grew moist, the candlelight seemed to expand, filling the room with a soft glow.

At that moment, far away, the old Bishop of Assisi, on a pilgrimage to Saint Michael, had a vision in which Francis said to him, "Behold, Father, I am leaving the world and I go to Christ."

One of the brothers outside the chapel reported seeing the soul of Francis, "like a star, but with the immensity of the moon and the brightness of the sun, ascending over many waters and borne aloft on a little white cloud, going directly to heaven."

Their "light" was gone.

Elias and Bernard did as Francis had asked, leaving him naked on the cold floor for "as long as it would take a man to walk a mile." They then washed him, anointed him with spice, and dressed him in a habit cut from Giacoma's ash gray cloth, pinning over it some of the coarse burlap he usually wore.

Thomas says that Francis died at sunset on Sunday, October 4, 1226, although to our way of reckoning time it was Saturday, October 3, since, at the time, the new day began at 6:00 p.m. rather than midnight.

Elias led in Brother Giacoma, who broke into tears. They took the body of Francis and placed him in her arms. "See," said the vicar, "he who you loved in life you shall hold in your arms in death." If the *Pieta* had already been formed by Michelangelo's hand, this scene would have mimicked it. She kissed Francis. He was covered with the ashen-colored cloth she had brought with her and his head was lying on her pillow, his face covered with her cloth. The body was also ornamented with five pearls. She could not help but see the stigmata and advised Elias that this miracle should no longer be hidden from the world.

With the room now ringed in the candles she had brought, the remainder of the brothers came quickly to him and kissed the hands and feet of their departed father. Thomas wrote that whereas his skin had been dark, it was "now gleaming with a dazzling whiteness."

Now they all saw the imprint of the nails and the wound in his side. Thomas repeated what he had written about the stigmata at La Verna. The nails were not just the holes "but the nails themselves formed out of his flesh and retaining the blackness of iron, his right side red with blood."

The people of Assisi, as many who could fit, rushed in to see Francis, singing canticles of joy, perhaps even his Canticle of the Sun. The sight of the stigmata in Francis's flesh aroused gasps of awe and amazement.

The next morning the people of Assisi joined the clergy to

carry the body from where he had died to San Damiano, where Lady Clare and the handmaids of Christ were located. Lady Clare was herself very ill at the time and grieved that she had not been able to be with Francis at his death. She was soon to become bedridden for the rest of her life.

People took up branches of trees, olive in particular, and sang praises all the way to San Damiano. The protective iron grille was removed from the window through which the lady servants of Christ usually received communion and sometimes heard Francis speak to them. The people lifted his body from the stretcher, raised him in their arms, and held him in front of the window for more than an hour. The women of San Damiano mourned tearfully as they kissed his hands, which wore precious gems and pearls.

The procession then moved on up the road into the city of Assisi, and they placed the body in the church of San Giorgio, where he had gone to school.[10] During his last months, Francis had made friends with a crow. It became fiercely loyal to him, sitting next to him at meals and accompanying him on his visits to the sick. When Francis died the crow followed his coffin to San Giorgio. It remained there, refusing to eat or to leave, and soon died.

EPILOGUE

The day of canonization for Francis was set for July 16, 1228, in the second year of Gregory IX's papacy. Pope Gregory, who ascended to the papacy following the death of Pope Honorius III, was actually Ugolino, the former bishop of Ostia, representative of the church for the order and friend of Francis.

On that day, abbots, bishops, cardinals, prelates from remote places, a king, and many counts and princes entered the city of Assisi "amid great pomp." The people of the city, *maiore* and *minore*, poured out into the streets and into the piazza before San Giorgio.

The pope wore gilded clothing covered with engraved jewels, while the cardinals were clad in splendid necklaces and white garments. The pope preached and praised Francis in what Thomas describes as "a noble eulogy with tears." Among his words were the following: "He shone in his days as the morning star in the midst of a cloud and as the moon at the full. And as the sun when it shines, so did he shine in the temple of God."[1]

After the pope's sermon and eulogy were finished, one of the pope's subdeacons, named Octavian, read the miracles of the saint before all in a very loud voice. A new flood of miracles began to be announced soon after the death of Francis. Miracles were said to have occurred at his tomb and still others when people merely called upon his name. In one miracle, a woman possessed by a demon had a vision of Francis telling her to make the sign of the cross.

Following the reading of the miracles, many songs were sung and praises offered in honor of the life of Francis. As a final tribute the pope kissed the tomb.

After the canonization, the pope laid the first stone for the new church to be built in honor of Francis. Among the things the pope donated for the new church was a golden cross, decorated with precious gems and containing wood reportedly from the Lord's cross.

The controversy over the difficulty of Francis's rules did not abate after his death, leaving the order in continued turmoil, while outside the order, the stigmata became a political firestorm.

Immediately following the death of Francis, Elias sent out an encyclical letter that, besides announcing Francis's death, contained the following revelation: "I announce to you a new miracle. . . . Not long before his death, our Brother and Father appeared crucified, bearing in his body five wounds—the stigmata of Christ. His hands and feet had been punctured right through as if by nails and still bore scars which had the blackness of nails. His side looked as if it had been pierced by a lance and often shed blood."[2]

There had been no precedent for such a thing and the leaders of the church did not know how to deal with it. It took ten years even for Gregory IX to accept the miracle of the stigmata. He may have been sincerely convinced by the outbreak of miracles that followed Francis's death and his new role as an intercessor, or his support may have been influenced by political necessity.

The conflict between the power of the papacy and the

emperor, Frederick II, provoked a rebellion in Rome that forced Pope Gregory and the curia to flee the city for most of five years, from 1230 to 1235. They moved first to Rieti and then were forced, by further conflict, to move farther from Rome—to Perugia.

The pope was, as a result, seeking allies. Both the Dominicans and the Franciscans were expanding, but they had become rivals with the Dominicans trying to distract attention from the miracle of the stigmata. At the same time, Francis's *Testament*, written shortly before his death, had further inflamed the wrangling over the rules. The pope wanted to end both the rivalry and the internal discord that were weakening the Franciscans.

In this process the dual controversies over the rules and the stigmata merged into a single defining debate over the exact nature of those wounds on Francis's body. Elias, in his encyclical, described the marks of the body of Francis to be "holes of nails." Thomas of Celano, as we have noted, however, emphasized that the nails in Francis were not holes but the actual nails become flesh. This is significant, for it made the nails part of Francis's body. Thomas also records that the threefold opening of the book landed on Luke 22:42–45 in which Jesus was in the Garden of Olives asking God to remove the cup of which he was about to take. The parallel is clear: Like Jesus in the garden, Francis was on Mount La Verna faced with the suffering that lay before him. The moment that the vision of the seraph disappeared, the memory of the Mount of Olives was so close to Francis that it brought out nails of flesh, copies of the nails of the cross. The appearance of the stigmata can therefore be regarded as arising from Francis's own actions.

Thomas also wrote, however, that the stigmata appeared

when the seraph disappeared—at a distinct moment. This gave rise to the argument that if the appearance of the stigmata actually appeared the specific instant when the seraph disappeared, then they were produced not by Francis in his extreme empathy with Christ but by divine intervention and were a singular event not accessible to anyone else.

To emphasize this point Bonaventure, in his biography on Francis, sets the threefold opening of the book to the scene of the Passion rather than in the garden. This detail suggests that, at La Verna, Francis was not absorbed in contemplating the different moments of the Passion and trying to relive the suffering of Christ in a spiritual fervor that might produce the wounds. Francis was, instead, contemplating the divine love that brought about the sacrifice of Jesus[3] and in that frame of mind received the wounds by the intervention of God himself.

The result of this murky reasoning was that Francis became elevated by a divine act beyond that attainable by mortal humans. Francis's level of sanctity was therefore inaccessible, and the brothers could choose a less demanding rule of life.

Four years after Francis's death and two years after his canonization, the bull *Quo elongati* promulgated by Gregory IX on September 28, 1230, deprived Francis's *Testament* of its status as a binding work that complemented the rule.

To reduce the dissension regarding the stigmata, extreme measures were taken. Bonaventure convinced the general chapter in Paris in 1266 to declare that the biography he had written be the only official biography of Francis. All other biographies were ordered to be destroyed. Thankfully, a few survived to be discovered later.

CONCLUSION

The fame of Francis over the centuries has grown to iconic proportions. In particular his love for birds and animals of every kind has endeared him to people of all faiths for eight centuries, encouraging people to neither exploit nor ignore the creatures with which we share this world. Lynn White, professor of history at the University of California, who blamed the world's ecological crisis largely on the prevailing concept of man's dominion over nature, wrote the following in a 1967 issue of *Science* magazine: "The greatest spiritual revolutionary in Western history, Saint Francis, proposed an alternative Christian view of nature and man's relation to it: he tried to substitute the idea of the equality of all creatures, including man, for the idea of man's limitless rule of creation. . . . I propose Francis as a patron saint for ecologists."[1]

There is no question that Francis perceived a profound connection among all living things. He would have undoubtedly appended the law "love your neighbor as yourself" to include "and care for all living things as fellow children of God." Some of his practices, like his insistence that no trees be completely chopped down so that they would be able to sprout, have many echoes today in the efforts of ecologists. But it is impossible to separate his love of nature from his certainty of God's overwhelming love. Every living creature—all the beauty of creation—he saw as an expression of that love.

In extolling Francis's ecological virtues, Professor White also refers to him as "the greatest spiritual revolutionary in Western history." Although most people, coming from various religious or nonreligious backgrounds, may have issues with some of his doctrines, rules, and practices, there is no question that Francis did have an astounding effect upon the faith of the people of his time. He revived a demoralized priesthood and brought new life to a spiritually barren society. In spite of the harsh rigors of his life, people flocked into the order—some giving up great wealth, power, and fame—to gain something of great value beyond the corporeal.

His message was not theologically profound; it was really quite simple: repent (or do penance) for the evils you have done, turn from your old life, and live in love and praise of the Lord. What made his message particularly appealing, though, was the way he presented it. Unlike so many before and so many down through the ages, he spoke without having a hidden personal agenda. This was one of the most powerful outgrowths of the order's devotion to poverty. The corruption of the church was apparent everywhere. Cardinals lived in palaces; bishops sold indulgences; evangelists sought the fame of a large following; and priests were openly promiscuous, more interested in obtaining wealth, power, or pleasure than in teaching the Christian faith. Everyone seemed to have an ulterior motive and their words, even the kind ones, were often perceived with suspicion.

A person standing before you attired in rags and refusing any kind of payment, gift, favor, or personal following is a message without words. Once madness and heresy could be ruled out, and people realized that the friars minor "had nothing" and truly "wanted nothing," the simplicity of their message and the raw power and sincerity of their faith was like a spring of water in a burning wasteland.

There were, of course, other messages that could be derived from Francis's devotion to poverty. Drawing attention to the plight of the poor is one that is often brought up. His concern and care for the poor, even the severely shunned lepers, could not help but be a powerful example, yet, while he encouraged people to give to the poor, he did not make it a political issue. The reason, in part, was that his was an age before entitlement programs when people were expected to accept the judgment of God for their conditions.

More important to Francis was the focus his choice of poverty placed upon what he considered to be truly valuable in life. That statement, to be sure, has become so encrusted with decades of clichés and sentimental portrayals in books, plays, movies, and sermons that it has almost lost all impact. On some level of thought, this may show that most people at least sense that the tendency to measure the value of human life in terms of physical possessions, financial success, or "personal worth" is a fallacy, one that objectifies children and devalues marriage, while burdening many with undue expectations and giving a false sense of importance to others.

Francis, himself a victim of his father's greed, dealt with this fallacy, not through verbal clichés and sentimental displays, but through vivid personal example. Most people probably believe that he pushed poverty to impossible levels and find themselves with divided loyalties in Francis's struggle against the brothers who sought to ease the rules. Yet he was also right. Ownership brings with it demands to protect and maintain that which we possess.

Francis believed that things separate us from God, or more correctly, our preoccupation with things does. He argues that our minds become so littered that we cannot see the most valuable entity of all—that "pearl of great price," which Francis identifies as the presence of God. To a people who had become more accustomed to fearing the punishment of God than to perceiving his goodness, this was an almost overwhelming revelation.

Any attempt to contemplate the life of Francis opens up many perspectives on life—on the self, human relations, religion, Christ, God, poverty, nature, and the meaning of life, among others. There are, however, problems associated with following in the footsteps of a saint. Once the word *saint* is attached to a name, that person's connection with humanity is severed. A saint is beyond human—existing somewhere between angelic realms and the heights of divinity. What the saint attained is not necessarily attainable for mortal beings. Just as Francis's *Testament* was ruled nonbinding because its precepts were ruled as being achievable only by a saint, his example is all too easily lost.

Francis, however, was definitively human. He was not only fallible, he spent much of his life in wanton self-indulgence. He was a braggart, ever boasting about the fame and glory he expected to achieve; a warrior, willing to shed blood in the pursuit of that glory; mischievous, willing to take advantage of others; a gang leader who may have engaged in street fights;

and a criminal, perhaps engaging in minor acts of thievery. His transformation is therefore a powerful testimony to the concept that God is approachable for even the most "lowly of sinners," as Francis often termed himself.

There is a remarkable consistency in the descriptions of how Francis encountered his Lord. They defied standard portrayals of piety and flew in the face of traditional religious practices. He didn't just utter words or emit a stream of carefully formed sentences. His prayers were not mere acts of communication; they were a joining with the divine. He prayed with a quiet intensity that could span the galaxies. Nothing was withheld; every aspect of his being—body, mind, and soul—leapt out in search of that divine spark.

There he found tenderness and joy, and, as if some chemical reaction had ensued, he "glowed" with the presence of God— an aura that stayed with him after he left his place of solitude, that followed him into the crowds of the city, that he often felt the need to hide lest it draw too much attention and make him a victim of vain congratulations. He pursued God in prayer, not because he had to, but because it filled his life more than food or water or the air he breathed.

Giosuè Alessandro Michele Carducci (1835–1907) was an Italian poet and teacher known for his hatred of Christianity and of the Catholic Church in particular. Among his poems is one entitled "Hymn to Satan." Yet this enemy of Christianity had a high regard for Francis. He wrote to a friend after returning from the shrine of Assisi, "I would like to knock on the gate of the Convent at Assisi, and to the little friar asking what I want, answer, like Dante, 'Peace.' . . . O holy Father St. Francis, if you who were so good that you converted even the wolf . . . if you were alive and interceded for me, who knows if even I would not be converted. . . . O Seraphic Father, if you were alive, I would confess to you . . . and then we would sing some Praises together."[2]

Nine years later Carducci wrote this fourteen-line tribute to Francis:

Santa Maria degli Angeli

How spacious, brother Francis, and how high
Is this fair dome of il Vignola spread
Above the spot where thou in agony
Layed'st naked with crossed arms, the earth thy bed!
Tis hot July : and o'er the plain, long wed
To labour, floats the love-song. Would that I
Caught in the Umbrian song thy accent sped,
Thy face reflected in the Umbrian sky!
And where the mountain-village stands outlined
'Gainst heav'n, a mild, lone radiance o'er thee poured,
As from thy Paradise that openeth,
Would I could see thee—arms outstretched and mind
Intent on God—singing: "Praised be the Lord
For death of the body, our dear sister Death."[3]

NOTES

CHAPTER 1: OUT OF THE NIGHT

1. Chiara Frugoni and Arsenio Frugoni, *A Day in a Medieval City* (Chicago: Univ. of Chicago Press, 2005), 45, 48.
2. Ibid., 8, 63.
3. Wendy Murray, *A Mended and Broken Heart* (New York: Perseus Books Group, 2008), 46.

CHAPTER 2: THE MERCHANT AND THE DREAMER

1. Thomas of Celano, *The Lives of S. Francis of Assisi*, trans. G. Ferrers Howell (London: Methuen & Co., 1908), 3–4.
2. Chiara Frugoni and Arsenio Frugoni, *A Day in a Medieval City* (Chicago: Univ. of Chicago Press, 2005), 128, 133; Brother Leo, *The Legend of the Three Companions*, edited by Regis J. Armstrong, et al. Vol. 2. 3 vols. (Hyde Park, NY: New City Press, 2000), 73.
3. Frugoni and Frugoni, *Day in a Medieval City*, 6–7, 49, 57, 63–64.
4. Ibid., 51.
5. Linda Bird Francke, *On the Road with Francis of Assisi* (New York: Random House, 2006), 9; Adrian House, *Francis of Assisi: A Revolutionary Life* (New York: Hidden Spring, 2003), 14.
6. Frugoni and Frugoni, *A Day in a Medieval City*, 137, 147.
7. Arnaldo Fortini and Helen Moak, *Francis of Assisi* (New York: Crossroad, 1992), 92.
8. Ian Campbell Ross, *Umbria: A Cultural History* (New York: Viking, 1996), 97.
9. Ferdinand Gregorovius, *History of the City of Rome in the Middle Ages* (London: G. Bell, 1897), 659–60.
10. Thomas of Celano, *The Second Life of St. Francis*, edited by Marian Habig, 1960 ed. (Chicago: Franciscan Herald Press, 1983), 373.
11. Fortini and Moak, *Francis of Assisi*, 84; Thomas of Celano, *Second Life*, 373.
12. Angus MacKay and David Ditchburn, *Atlas of Medieval Europe* (New York: Routledge, 1997), 129.

CHAPTER 3: THE PLAYBOY

1. Konrad Eisenbichler, *The Premodern Teenager* (Toronto: Centre for Reformation and Renaissance Studies, 2002), 30.

2. Thomas of Celano, *The Second Life of St. Francis*, edited by Marian Habig, 1960 ed. (Chicago: Franciscan Herald Press, 1983), 363.

3. Brother Leo, *The Legend of the Three Companions*, edited by Regis J. Armstrong, et al. Vol. 2. 3 vols. (Hyde Park, NY: New City Press, 2000), 68.

4. Arnaldo Fortini and Helen Moak, *Francis of Assisi* (New York: Crossroad, 1992), 136.

5. Chiara Frugoni and Arsenio Frugoni, *A Day in a Medieval City* (Chicago: Univ. of Chicago Press, 2005), 126.

6. Eisenbichler, *Premodern Teenager*, 305.

7. Ibid., 293.

8. Wendy Murray, *A Mended and Broken Heart* (New York: Perseus Books Group, 2008), 95–96.

9. Thomas of Celano, *The Lives of S. Francis of Assisi*, trans. G. Ferrers Howell (London: Methuen & Co., 1908), 4.

10. William Heywood and Robert Langton Douglas, *A History of Perugia* (New York: G. P. Putnam's Sons, 1910), 90.

CHAPTER 4: THE KNIGHT OF ASSISI

1. Ian Campbell Ross, *Umbria: A Cultural History* (New York: Viking, 1996), 68–72.

2. Arnaldo Fortini and Helen Moak, *Francis of Assisi* (New York: Crossroad, 1992), 141–42.

3. Chiara Frugoni, *Francis of Assisi* (New York: Continuum, 1998), 82.

4. Adrian House, *Francis of Assisi: A Revolutionary Life* (New York: Hidden Spring, 2003), 19–20.

5. Fortini and Moak, *Francis of Assisi*, 73.

6. Linda Bird Francke, *On the Road with Francis of Assisi* (New York: Random House, 2006), 12.

7. Ferdinand Gregorovius, *History of the City of Rome in the Middle Ages* (London: G. Bell, 1897), 598.

8. House, *Francis of Assisi*, 42.

9. Brother Leo, *The Legend of the Three Companions*, edited by Regis J. Armstrong, et al. Vol. 2. 3 vols. (Hyde Park, NY: New City Press,

2000), 70; Thomas of Celano, *The Lives of S. Francis of Assisi*, trans. G. Ferrers Howell (London: Methuen & Co., 1908), 364.

10. House, *Francis of Assisi*, 44, 81.

Chapter 5: From Riches to Rags

1. Thomas of Celano, *The Lives of S. Francis of Assisi*, trans. G. Ferrers Howell (London: Methuen & Co., 1908), 5.

2. Ian Campbell Ross, *Umbria: A Cultural History* (New York: Viking, 1996), 6–7; Adrian House, *Francis of Assisi: A Revolutionary Life* (New York: Hidden Spring, 2003), 27, 29.

3. Thomas of Celano, *Lives*, 5.

4. Arnaldo Fortini and Helen Moak, *Francis of Assisi* (New York: Crossroad, 1992), 167.

5. Brother Leo, *The Legend of the Three Companions*, edited by Regis J. Armstrong, et al. Vol. 2. 3 vols. (Hyde Park, NY: New City Press, 2000), 70.

6. Thomas of Celano, *Lives*, 7.

7. Brother Leo, *Three Companions*, 23.

8. House, *Francis of Assisi*, 48, 50.

9. Brother Leo, *Three Companions*, 72.

10. Wendy Murray, *A Mended and Broken Heart* (New York: Perseus Books Group, 2008), 46.

11. Brother Leo, *Three Companions*, 73.

12. Ferdinand Gregorovius, *History of the City of Rome in the Middle Ages* (London: G. Bell, 1897), 658–59.

13. Marilyn Stokstad, *Medieval Art* (Boulder, CO: Westview Press, 2004), 31.

14. Thomas of Celano, *The Second Life of St. Francis*, edited by Marian Habig, 1960 ed. (Chicago: Franciscan Herald Press, 1983), 368; Brother Leo, *Three Companions*, 73.

Chapter 6: A New Light

1. Brother Leo, *The Legend of the Three Companions*, Edited by Regis J. Armstrong, et al. Vol. 2. 3 vols. (Hyde Park, NY: New City Press, 2000), 72.

2. Ibid., 74.

3. Wendy Murray, *A Mended and Broken Heart* (New York: Perseus Books Group, 2008), 82–83.

4. Francis of Assisi, *Testament*.

5. Brother Leo, *Three Companions*, 75; Thomas of Celano, *The Lives of S. Francis of Assisi*, trans. G. Ferrers Howell (London: Methuen & Co., 1908), 8.

6. Brother Leo, *Three Companions*, 75.

7. Thomas of Celano, *Lives*, 12; Brother Leo, *Three Companions*, 78.

CHAPTER 7: THE CHRYSALIS BREAKS

1. Wendy Murray, *A Mended and Broken Heart* (New York: Perseus Books Group, 2008), 58.

2. Thomas of Celano, *The Lives of S. Francis of Assisi*, trans. G. Ferrers Howell (London: Methuen & Co., 1908), 12.

3. Murray, *Mended and Broken Heart*, 58.

4. Thomas of Celano, *Lives*, 12.

5. Brother Leo, *The Legend of the Three Companions*, edited by Regis J. Armstrong, et al. Vol. 2. 3 vols. (Hyde Park, NY: New City Press, 2000), 78.

6. Thomas of Celano, *Lives*, 13–15; Brother Leo, *Three Companions*, 79.

7. Brother Leo, *Three Companions*, 79.

8. Murray, *Mended and Broken Heart*, 62.

9. Thomas of Celano, *The Second Life of St. Francis*, edited by Marian Habig, 1960 ed. (Chicago: Franciscan Herald Press, 1983), 372; Brother Leo, *Three Companions*, 80.

10. Thomas of Celano, *Lives*, 17.

11. Murray, *Mended and Broken Heart*, 68.

CHAPTER 8: RAGTAG BROTHERS

1. Brother Leo, *The Legend of the Three Companions*, edited by Regis J. Armstrong, et al. Vol. 2. 3 vols. (Hyde Park, NY: New City Press, 2000), 81.

2. Ibid., 82.

3. Thomas of Celano, *The Second Life of St. Francis*, Edited by Marian Habig, 1960 ed. (Chicago: Franciscan Herald Press, 1983), 373; Brother Leo, *Three Companions*, 83.

4. Wendy Murray, *A Mended and Broken Heart* (New York: Perseus Books Group, 2008), 73; Brother Leo, *Three Companions*, 83.

5. Adrian House, *Francis of Assisi: A Revolutionary Life* (New York: Hidden Spring, 2003), 80.

6. Thomas of Celano, *The Lives of S. Francis of Assisi*, trans. G. Ferrers Howell (London: Methuen & Co., 1908), 24; Brother Leo, *Three Companions*, 85.

7. Murray, *Mended and Broken Heart*, 75.

8. Brother Leo, *Three Companions*, 86–87.

9. Arnaldo Fortini and Helen Moak, *Francis of Assisi* (New York: Crossroad, 1992), 279–80.

10. Brother Leo, *Three Companions*, 91–92.

11. Ibid., 89.

12. Fortini and Moak, *Francis of Assisi*, 26.

13. Brother Leo, *Three Companions*, 94–95

CHAPTER 9: THE ROAD TO DESTINY

1. Thomas of Celano, *The Lives of S. Francis of Assisi*, trans. G. Ferrers Howell (London: Methuen & Co., 1908), 31–32; Brother Leo, *The Legend of the Three Companions*, edited by Regis J. Armstrong, et al. Vol. 2. 3 vols. (Hyde Park, NY: New City Press, 2000), 95–96.

2. Brother Leo, *Three Companions*, 96.

3. Arnaldo Fortini and Helen Moak, *Francis of Assisi* (New York: Crossroad, 1992), 252.

4. Caecilia Davis-Weyer, *Early Medieval Art, 300–1150* (Toronto: Univ. of Toronto Press, 1986), 89–90.

5. Rosalind B. Brooke, *The Image of St Francis* (New York: Cambridge Univ. Press, 2006), 193.

6. Ibid.

7. Bonaventure, *The Major Life of St. Francis of Assisi (from the Legenda Sancti Francisci)*,. edited by Marian Habig, 4th ed. (Chicago: Franciscan Herald Press, 1983), 651.

8. Thomas of Celano, *The Second Life of St. Francis*, edited by Marian Habig, 1960 ed. (Chicago: Franciscan Herald Press, 1983), 376–77; John of Perugia, *Leg. of Perugia*, 50; Brother Leo, *Three Companions*, 97.

9. Bonaventure, *Major Life*, 651.

10. Brother Leo, *Three Companions*, 97–98.

11. Brother Leo, *Three Companions*, 96.

12. Father Paschal Robinson, trans., *The Writings of St. Francis of Assisi* (Philadelphia: The Dolphin Press, 1905), 46.

13. Thomas of Celano, *Lives*, 34–35, 39.

14. Brother Leo, *Three Companions*, 99; Adrian House, *Francis of Assisi: A Revolutionary Life* (New York: Hidden Spring, 2003), 101.

15. Thomas of Celano, *Lives*, 43.

16. Brother Leo, *Three Companions*, 99–100.

CHAPTER 10: THE POVERELLO AND THE FRIARS MINOR

1. Francis of Assisi, "First Rule," 34.

2. Thomas of Celano, *The Second Life of St. Francis*, edited by Marian Habig, 1960 ed. (Chicago: Franciscan Herald Press, 1983), 72.

3. Ibid., 91.

4. Thomas of Celano, *The Lives of S. Francis of Assisi*, trans. G. Ferrers Howell (London: Methuen & Co., 1908), 40, 42, 52; Adrian House, *Francis of Assisi: A Revolutionary Life* (New York: Hidden Spring, 2003), 105.

5. Francis of Assisi, "First Rule," 43.

6. Francis of Assisi, "First Rule," 43; John of Perugia, *Leg. of Perugia*, 151.

7. Arnaldo Fortini and Helen Moak, *Francis of Assisi* (New York: Crossroad, 1992), 73.

8. Francis of Assisi, "First Rule," 33, 42.

9. Charles George Herbermann, *The Catholic Encyclopedia* (New York: Universal Knowledge Foundation, 1913), 768–69.

10. Thomas of Celano, *Second Life*, 152.

11. Ibid., 83.

12. Ibid., 22, 129.

13. Thomas of Celano, *Lives*, 54; Thomas of Celano, *Second Life*, 133.

14. Francis of Assisi, "Admonitions."

15. Thomas of Celano, *First Life of St. Francis*, edited by Marian Habig, 1960 ed. (Chicago Franciscan Herald Press, 1983), Francis of Assisi, "First Rule," 38.

16. Thomas of Celano, *Second Life*, 83.

17. Thomas of Celano, *Lives*, 18.

CHAPTER 11: CLARE: LADY OF LIGHT

1. Wendy Murray, *A Mended and Broken Heart* (New York: Perseus Books Group, 2008), 11, 43.

2. Ibid., 44.

3. Chiara Frugoni, *Francis of Assisi* (New York: Continuum, 1998), 51.

4. Thomas of Celano, *The Second Life of St. Francis*, edited by Marian Habig, 1960 ed. (Chicago: Franciscan Herald Press, 1983), 91, 95–96.
5. Murray, *Mended and Broken Heart*, 94.
6. Thomas of Celano, *The Lives of S. Francis of Assisi*, trans. G. Ferrers Howell (London: Methuen & Co., 1908), 19–20.
7. Arnaldo Fortini and Helen Moak, *Francis of Assisi* (New York: Crossroad, 1992), 128.

CHAPTER 12: A VOICE IN THE WILDERNESS

1. Thomas of Celano, *The Second Life of St. Francis*, edited by Marian Habig, 1960 ed. (Chicago: Franciscan Herald Press, 1983), 83.
2. *The Little Flowers of Saint Francis of Assisi*, edited by Marian Habig, 1960 ed. (Chicago: Franciscan Herald Press, 1983), 1322-23.
3. Thomas of Celano, *Second Life*, 72, 163.
4. Thomas of Celano, *The Lives of S. Francis of Assisi*, trans. G. Ferrers Howell (London: Methuen & Co., 1908), 73.
5. Thomas of Celano, *Second Life*, 146.
6. Francis of Assisi, "Admonitions," 18.
7. Thomas of Celano, *Second Life*, 45, 61, 94–95.
8. Ibid., 99.
9. Ibid., 95.
10. Ibid., 127.

CHAPTER 13: GROWING PAINS

1. Arnaldo Fortini and Helen Moak, *Francis of Assisi* (New York: Crossroad, 1992), 82–83.
2. Thomas of Celano, *The Lives of S. Francis of Assisi*, trans. G. Ferrers Howell (London: Methuen & Co., 1908), 37.
3. Adrian House, *Francis of Assisi: A Revolutionary Life* (New York: Hidden Spring, 2003), 143–44; Thomas of Celano, *First Life of St. Francis*, edited by Marian Habig, 1960 ed. (Chicago: Franciscan Herald Press, 1983), 56.
4. John of Perugia, *Leg. of Perugia*, 54–55; Brother Leo, *The Legend of the Three Companions*, edited by Regis J. Armstrong, et al. Vol. 2. 3 vols. (Hyde Park, NY: New City Press, 2000), 103.
5. Wendy Murray, *A Mended and Broken Heart* (New York: Perseus Books Group, 2008), 112.
6. Thomas of Celano, *First Life*, 290–91.

7. *St. Francis of Assisi: Writings and Early Biographies: English Omnibus of the Sources for the Life of St. Francis*, edited by Marian Habig, 4th ed. (Chicago: Franciscan Herald Press, 1983), 1608.

8. Chiara Frugoni, *Francis of Assisi* (New York: Continuum, 1998), 62.

CHAPTER 14: LEGEND

1. Thomas of Celano, *The Second Life of St. Francis*, edited by Marian Habig, 1960 ed. (Chicago: Franciscan Herald Press, 1983), 59.

2. Thomas of Celano, *First Life of St. Francis*, edited by Marian Habig, 1960 ed. (Chicago: Franciscan Herald Press, 1983), 278.

3. Thomas of Celano, *Second Life*, 165, 200.

4. Thomas of Celano, *First Life*, 296; Thomas of Celano, *The Lives of S. Francis of Assisi*, trans. G. Ferrers Howell (London: Methuen & Co., 1908), 58.

5. Thomas of Celano, *Lives*, 65.

6. *The Little Flowers of Saint Francis of Assisi*, trans. Thomas Okey (London: Burns Oates & Washbourne Ltd., n.d.), 27–29.

CHAPTER 15: THE KNIGHT OF CHRIST

1. Wendy Murray, *A Mended and Broken Heart* (New York: Perseus Books Group, 2008), 110.

2. Thomas F. Madden, *The New Concise History of the Crusades* (Lanham, MD: Rowman & Littlefield, 2005), 108–9.

3. David Nicolle and Graham Turner, *Acre 1291* (New York: Osprey Publishing, 2005), 8; Murray, *A Mended and Broken Heart*, 113–14.

4. Murray, *A Mended and Broken Heart*, 113.

5. Thomas of Celano, *The Second Life of St. Francis*, edited by Marian Habig, 1960 ed. (Chicago: Franciscan Herald Press, 1983), 30.

6. Steven Runciman, *A History of the Crusades: Volume 3, The Kingdom of Acre and the Later Crusades* (New York: Cambridge Univ. Press, 1954), 159.

7. Ibid., 159–60.

8. Thomas of Celano, *The Lives of S. Francis of Assisi*, trans. G. Ferrers Howell (London: Methuen & Co., 1908), 57.

9. Bonaventure, *The Major Life of St. Francis of Assisi (from the Legenda Sancti Francisci)*, edited by Marian Habig, 4th ed. (Chicago: Franciscan Herald Press, 1983), 705.

CHAPTER 16: DIVISIONS AND REPERCUSSIONS

1. Brother Leo, *The Legend of the Three Companions*, edited by Regis J. Armstrong, et al. Vol. 2. 3 vols. (Hyde Park, NY: New City Press, 2000), 105.
2. Thomas of Celano, *The Second Life of St. Francis*, edited by Marian Habig, 1960 ed. (Chicago: Franciscan Herald Press, 1983), 58.
3. Ibid., 75.
4. Thomas of Celano, *First Life of St. Francis*, edited by Marian Habig, 1960 ed. (Chicago: Franciscan Herald Press, 1983), 103.
5. John of Perugia, *Leg. of Perugia*, 76.
6. Francis of Assisi, *Testament*, 85.
7. Thomas of Celano, *Second Life*, 69.
8. Ibid., 188.
9. *The Little Flower of Saint Francis of Assisi*, edited by Marian Habig, 1960 ed. (Chicago: Franciscan Herald Press, 1983), 1340.
10. John of Perugia, *Leg. of Perugia*, 14.
11. *St. Francis of Assisi: Writings and Early Biographies: English Omnibus of the Sources for the Life of St. Francis*, edited by Marian Habig, 4th ed. (Chicago: Franciscan Herald Press, 1983), 1601–2.
12. John of Perugia, *Leg. of Perugia*, 74.
13. Thomas of Celano, *Second Life*, 119–20, 197.
14. Ibid., 123.

CHAPTER 17: MIRACLES IN THE SHADOW OF DEATH

1. Thomas of Celano, *First Life of St. Francis*, edited by Marian Habig, 1960 ed. (Chicago: Franciscan Herald Press, 1983), 86.
2. Ibid., 85.
3. *The Little Flowers of Saint Francis of Assisi*, edited by Marian Habig, 1960 ed. (Chicago: Franciscan Herald Press, 1983), 1434.
4. Thomas of Celano, *First Life*, 91.
5. *Little Flowers of Saint Francis*, edited by Marian Habig, 1434.
6. Adrian House, *Francis of Assisi: A Revolutionary Life* (New York: Hidden Spring, 2003), 257.
7. Thomas of Celano, *First Life*, 95.
8. Paul Sabatier, *Life of St. Francis of Assisi*, trans. Louise Seymour Houghton (New York: C. Scribner's Sons, 1894), 300.
9. *St. Francis of Assisi: Writings and Early Biographies: English Omnibus of the Sources for the Life of St. Francis*, edited by Marian

    Habig, 4th ed. (Chicago: Franciscan Herald Press, 1983), 130–31.
10. Thomas of Celano, *The Second Life of St. Francis*, edited by Marian
    Habig, 1960 ed. (Chicago: Franciscan Herald Press, 1983), 126.
11. Thomas of Celano, *First Life*, 105.
12. House, *Francis of Assisi*, 276–77.

CHAPTER 18: LAST DAYS

 1. *St. Francis of Assisi: Writings and Early Biographies: English
    Omnibus of the Sources for the Life of St. Francis*, edited by Marian
    Habig, 4th ed. (Chicago: Franciscan Herald Press, 1983), 131.
 2. Thomas of Celano, *First Life of St. Francis*, edited by Marian Habig,
    1960 ed. (Chicago: Franciscan Herald Press, 1983), 108.
 3. Ibid., 106, 108.
 4. John of Perugia, *Leg. of Perugia*, 126.
 5. Ibid.
 6. Thomas of Celano, *First Life*, 107.
 7. Ibid., 109.
 8. Ibid., 116.
 9. Thomas of Celano, *The Second Life of St. Francis*, edited by Marian
    Habig, 1960 ed. (Chicago: Franciscan Herald Press, 1983), 214.
10. Thomas of Celano, *First Life*, 118.

EPILOGUE

 1. Thomas of Celano, *First Life of St. Francis*, Edited by Marian
    Habig, 1960 ed. (Chicago: Franciscan Herald Press, 1983), 125.
 2. *St. Francis of Assisi: Writings and Early Biographies: English
    Omnibus of the Sources for the Life of St. Francis*, edited by Marian
    Habig, 4th ed. (Chicago: Franciscan Herald Press, 1983), 1894.
 3. Chiara Frugoni, *Francis of Assisi* (New York: Continuum, 1998), 137–38.

CONCLUSION

 1. Lynn Townsend White Jr., "The Historical Roots of Our Ecologic
    Crisis," *Science* 155, number 3767: 1207.
 2. Quoted in Raphael Brown, *The Roots of St. Francis* (Chicago:
    Franciscan Herald Press, 1981), 62.
 3. Giosuè Carducci, *Carducci*, edited by G. L. Bickersteth (London:
    Longmans, Green, 1913), 141.

BIBLIOGRAPHY

Armstrong, Regis J., ed. *Francis of Assisi*. Translated by William J. Short and J. A. Wayne Hellmann. Hyde Park, NY: New City Press, 2001.

The Assisi Compilation (The Anonymous of Perugia), in *Francis of Assisi*. Edited by Regis J. Armstrong, et al. Vol. 2. 3 vols. Hyde Park, NY: New City Press, 2000.

Bonaventure. *The Major Life of St. Francis of Assisi (from the Legenda Sancti Francisci)*. Edited by Marian Habig. 4th ed. Chicago: Franciscan Herald Press, 1983.

Brooke, Rosalind B. *The Image of St Francis*. New York: Cambridge Univ. Press, 2006.

Brown, Raphael. *The Roots of St. Francis*. Chicago: Franciscan Herald Press, 1981.

Carducci, Giosuè. *Carducci*. Edited by G. L. Bickersteth. London: Longmans, Green, 1913.

Davis-Weyer, Caecilia. *Early Medieval Art, 300–1150*. Toronto: Univ. of Toronto Press, 1986.

Eisenbichler, Konrad. *The Premodern Teenager*. Toronto: Centre for Reformation and Renaissance Studies, 2002.

Fortini, Arnaldo, and Helen Moak. *Francis of Assisi*. New York: Crossroad, 1992.

Francis of Assisi. "Admonitions." Translated by Father Paschal Robinson, 1905.

———. "First Rule." Translated by Father Paschal Robinson, 1905.

———. *Testament*. Translated by Father Paschal Robinson, 1905.

Francke, Linda Bird. *On the Road with Francis of Assisi*. New York: Random House, Inc., 2006.

Frugoni, Chiara. *Francis of Assisi*. New York: Continuum, 1998.

Frugoni, Chiara, and Arsenio Frugoni. *A Day in a Medieval City*. Chicago: Univ. of Chicago Press, 2005.

Gregorovius, Ferdinand. *History of the City of Rome in the Middle Ages*. London: G. Bell, 1897.

Habig, Marion, ed. *The Little Flowers of Saint Francis of Assisi*. 1960 ed. Chicago: Franciscan Herald Press, 1983.

———. *St. Francis of Assisi: Writings and Early Biographies: English Omnibus*

of the Sources for the Life of St. Francis. 4th ed. Chicago: Franciscan
Herald Press, 1983.

Herbermann, Charles George. *The Catholic Encyclopedia*. New York:
Universal Knowledge Foundation, 1913.

Heywood, William, and Robert Langton Douglas. *A History of Perugia*. New
York: G. P. Putnam's Sons, 1910.

Hill, David Jayne. *A History of Diplomacy in the International Development of
Europe*. London: Longmans, Green, and Co., 1905.

House, Adrian. *Francis of Assisi: A Revolutionary Life*. New York: Hidden
Spring, 2003.

Brother Leo. *The Legend of the Three Companions*. Edited by Regis J.
Armstrong, et al. Vol. 2. 3 vols. Hyde Park, NY: New City Press, 2000.

The Little Flowers of Saint Francis of Assisi. Trans. Thomas Okey. London:
Burns Oates & Washbourne Ltd.

MacKay, Angus, and David Ditchburn. *Atlas of Medieval Europe*. New York:
Routledge, 1997.

Madden, Thomas F. *The New Concise History of the Crusades*. Lanham, MD:
Rowman & Littlefield, 2005.

Murray, Wendy. *A Mended and Broken Heart*. New York: Perseus Books
Group, 2008.

Newman, Paul B. *Daily Life in the Middle Ages*. Jefferson, NC: McFarland, 2001.

Nicolle, David, and Graham Turner. *Acre 1291*. New York: Osprey
Publishing, 2005.

Robinson, Father Paschal, trans. *The Writings of St. Francis of Assisi*.
Philadelphia: The Dolphin Press, 1905.

Robson, Michael. *St. Francis of Assisi*. London: Continuum International
Publishing Group, 1999.

Ross, Ian Campbell. *Umbria: A Cultural History*. New York: Viking, 1996.

Runciman, Steven. *A History of the Crusades: Volume 3, The Kingdom of Acre
and the Later Crusades*. New York: Cambridge Univ. Press, 1954.

Sabatier, Paul. *Life of St. Francis of Assisi*. Trans. Louise Seymour Houghton.
New York: C. Scribner's Sons, 1894.

Stokstad, Marilyn. *Medieval Art*. Boulder, CO: Westview Press, 2004.

Thomas of Celano. *First Life of St. Francis*. Edited by Marian Habig. 1960 ed.
Chicago: Franciscan Herald Press, 1983.

———. *The Lives of S. Francis of Assisi*. Trans. G. Ferrers Howell. London:
Methuen & Co., 1908.

———. *The Second Life of St. Francis*. Edited by Marian Habig. 1960 ed.
Chicago: Franciscan Herald Press, 1983.

White, Jr., Lynn Townsend. "The Historical Roots of Our Ecologic Crisis."
Science 155, no. 3767: 1203–07.

ABOUT THE AUTHOR

Robert West has been a university professor, an actor, a theater director, a stage designer, a screenwriter, an associate producer and/or story editor for several movies, and along the way, a husband and a father of three sons.